Gardening *with*
foliage, form *and* texture

Gardening *with* foliage, form *and* texture

Ethne Clarke

with photographs by Clive Nichols

David & Charles

A DAVID & CHARLES BOOK

First published in the UK in 1996
First paperback edition 2004

Copyright © David & Charles 1996, 2004
Text copyright © Ethne Clarke 1996, 2004
Photographs copyright © Clive Nichols except those acknowledged on page 160

Ethne Clarke has asserted her right to be identified as author of this work in accordance
with the Copyright, Designs and Patents Act, 1988.

This book was previously published by David & Charles as *Leaf, Bark and Berry*.

A catalogue record for this book is available from the British Library.

ISBN 0 7153 1811 X Paperback
ISBN 0 7153 6794 3 Hardback

Art Editor Micheal Whitehead
Illustrations Diana Leadbetter

Printed in Singapore by KHL Printing Co Pte Ltd
for David & Charles
Brunel House   Newton Abbot   Devon

Visit our website at www.davidandcharles.co.uk

David & Charles books are available from all good bookshops; alternatively you can contact our Orderline on (0)1626 334555
or write to us at FREEPOST EX2 110, David & Charles Direct, Newton Abbot, TQ12 4ZZ (no stamp required UK mainland).

CONTENTS

FOREWORD

FOLIAGE WAS NOT, I MUST ADMIT, MY FIRST INTEREST WHEN I began gardening. Flower colour was all and everything and hours were spent plotting Jekyllian schemes, which rarely made the transition from drawing pad to garden border, mostly because I would rather acquire one special plant than a dozen of a certain colour. In any case, I soon got tired of shouldering the responsibility of trying to orchestrate 'year-round' colour - something was always out of tune.

It was the Stream Garden at Hidcote that knocked the scales from my eyes. It is the lowest point in the topography of that splendid garden and the water in the little rivulet is completely obscured by an enormous range of equally enormous leaves. The contrasts of forms, leaf shapes and textures in this group of moisture-loving plants held my attention like no flower border had ever done. The backdrop was formed from the tight clipped hedges that characterize the garden layout at Hidcote, and the whole composition was suddenly revealed to me in layers of various tints of green, from cool silver to dark purples, browns and reds.

Foliage is the canvas upon which we paint our garden pictures. Green is the perfect foil for flower colour and the complex contrasts of form, shape and texture ease our gardens into the natural landscape.

Beth Chatto's Gold Medal-winning displays at the Chelsea Flower Show in 1987 was another turning point. Beth's credo rests on suiting the plant to the site rather than trying to adjust the site to accommodate the plant, and immaculate preparation of the soil. Her compositions are as carefully thought out as any painter's two-dimensional work, but the effect is entirely natural and uncontrived. This is best studied in her garden at Elmstead Market in Essex, and I soon beat a path to her gate determined to apply her techniques to my newly acquired empty field in central Norfolk. If you can't visit the Chatto garden, then I highly recommend her book, *The Green Tapestry*.

Pippa Rakusen, too, and her treasure-filled garden Lyng Beeches near Leeds, taught me much about the beauty of woodland gardening; she has been as generous with her knowledge as she has with cuttings, plants and seed, convinced that I could learn and that the plants were going to a good home - a real leap of faith on both counts! Her book *Foliage and Form Throughout the Year* was my first primer on the subject, and copies can be obtained by post or in person from the Northern Horticultural Society at Harlow Carr, Harrogate (the gardens are also worth a visit).

A visit to West Central Texas took me to Peckerwood Gardens where John Fairey relies on the blue-grey tints of fleshy-leaved succulents and sculptural agaves to visually cool down the view of the garden from the house. Dusk fell before he and Carl Schoenfeld had shown me the whole garden collection and the neighbouring Yucca Do nursery, so we carried on by moonlight under which the exotic plants took on an additional layer of glamour as they were reduced entirely to form and texture.

It was while working with Clive Nichols on my book about herb garden design that he and I determined to do a book which would present our enthusiasm for the brilliant design potential of foliage plants. We have both spent many years looking at plants and gardens, and increasingly it was the way in which foliage was used as the backbone of the garden which caused us the most excitement. We have tried to include as many of the fine leafed plants as we have enjoyed in our journeys through many different types of garden. Whether driven by the 'eco-habitat' gardens at the cutting edge of modern design or the more traditionally inspired formal gardens, all the gardeners mentioned in this book share an interest in growing foliage plants well in the situations that will suit them best. We are indebted to them for sharing their knowledge and gardens with us.

Nevertheless, I am quite sure many of your favourite foliage plants will be missing, or that some of my favourites wouldn't be looked at twice by someone else. Thankfully, the world is full of different opinions, and particularly the garden world, which is what makes gardening a lively topic of discussion and garden-visiting a major recreational sport. So, I hope you will take pleasure in the gardens and plant groupings shown here and find as much inspiration in them as I have done. And I hope that we will succeed in firing your passion for foliage, form and texture.

Ethne Clarke
Yaxham, Norfolk
March 1996

IN A GREEN GARDEN

*'Our country is one complete garden, each
section adding its chorus to the great symphony.'*
Siftings, *Jens Jensen, 1939.*

FOR CENTURIES WE HAVE BEEN CREATING GARDENS, TRYING to 'improve on nature' and exercise control over our environment. Gardeners have manipulated the lines of the natural terrain, altered the course of rivers or introduced water where it did not naturally exist. They have even gone so far as to create artificial environments – rockeries, peat gardens, bog gardens and the like – to nurture a garden full of colourful exotics. We are steeped in that tradition and to it have added our own lavish use of hard-landscaping features: stone walls, sweeping terraces, paved paths, electric fountains and waterfalls, artificial lighting and so on. Much of the display is intended to 'give the garden structure' and to retain interest after the flowers have faded.

However, there is another way for the garden to hold our attention throughout the year, a way of working with nature that allows for the development of a more relaxed and natural style of planting, and one that is more in harmony with our surroundings. There is no easier way to understand this approach than to step beyond your garden gate. Take

A formal garden of evergreen topiary frames the natural landscape of meadows and tree-lined streams which inspired the landscape architect Capability Brown to reject the artifice of formality and 'improve on nature' in his designs.

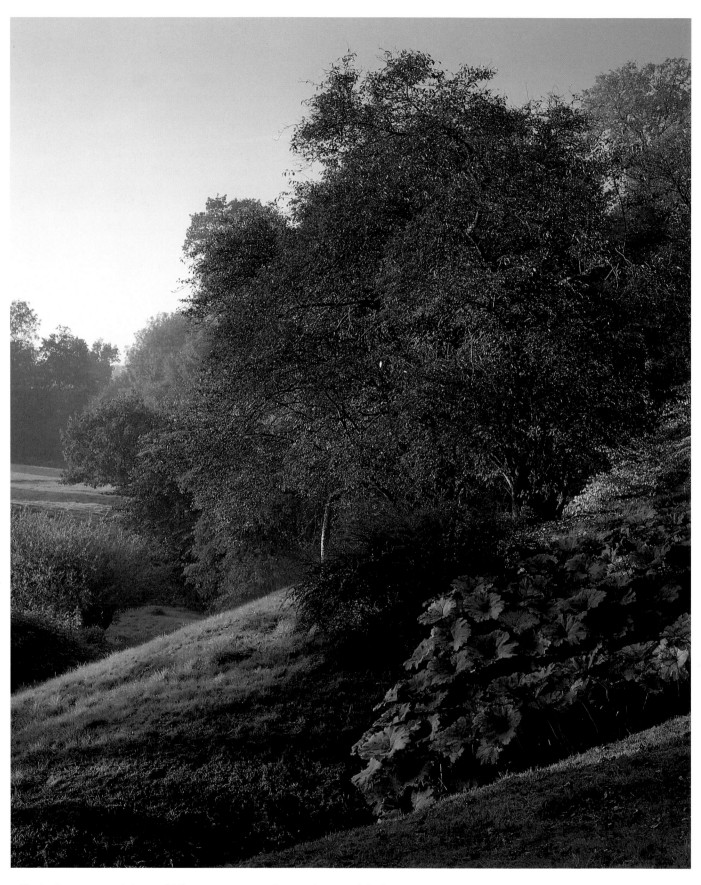

The landscape appears in layers of foliage: tree canopy, understory plantings of shrubs, perennials, annuals and groundcovers. These are also the basics of garden planting against which flower and berry colour comes and goes.

12

a good hard look at the natural landscape around you and the meaning of Jensen's words will become immediately apparent. If we regard the plants in our gardens as notes of music and ourselves as musicians, we should be studying how nature composes her symphonies and then trying to adapt her variations and repetitions of foliage colours, textures, forms and shapes to formulate the theme of our own garden.

Foliage is displayed in the natural landscape in layers and each layer imposes its own conditions on the environment. The primary layer is the tree canopy; beneath this layer are the shrubs and, lower still, the perennials and what I term 'ephemerals', the annual and biennial tribe. At the bottom are the groundcovers, which include plants from the shrub and the perennial groups. These layers interact, creating a variety of growing conditions, such as the deep shade cast by a stand of densely leaved trees, or damp soil as promoted by the use of groundcovering plants to conserve moisture. Follow nature and you are on the way to creating a garden where the harmonies of the seasons are captured in the repeated theme of beautiful leaves accented by the passing show of flowers and berry.

Shelters

Trees have the most immediate and obvious influence on our landscape because of their height and longevity, and the ways in which they are used in large part give the landscape its shape. First and foremost, trees are used to provide shelter belts and each region will have its own requirements, determined by climate. A windy coastal garden will benefit from a mixed screen of evergreens and deciduous trees to mitigate the effect of salt-laden breezes and cut wind speeds through the garden. An inland garden in a mild temperate zone would obtain sufficient benefit from a single row of deciduous trees whose trunks and branches would provide all the wind baffle needed.

The key to the success of a shelter belt relies less on which trees are used (although you should aim to use species that appear naturally in your area) than on the provision of a uniformly dense screen according to the degree of protection required. This can be either a wide plantation belt of evergreens, or a more open boundary of mixed deciduous trees which will

Deciduous trees like this *Aesculus* x *carnea* make a statement all year-round, from the moment the fresh green leaf buds burst to the moment they drop to spread a golden carpet on the ground.

allow light to filter through and so create the sensation of a woodland edge. Such a scheme could then be planted with shrubs and herbaceous perennials that would appreciate the low light and moist conditions such a tree planting would offer. Also, bear in mind that it is only necessary for a shelter belt to contain two or three species, which should be planted in clusters rather than uniform lines. Again, the best teacher is nature, so take a good look around.

When planning a shelter belt, there are various considerations. First, the seasonal wind directions. In my Norfolk garden in the east of England, the prevailing winds are from southwest to northeast during spring and summer, and then sweep around to northwest to southeast in the autumn and winter. This is not unlike the wind patterns of the prairies of the American Midwest which, curiously, Norfolk resembles in other ways, including the big blue skies and mega-fields (relatively speaking of course). Knowing this, I planted trees to shelter the garden from the worst of winter's Siberian winds, and to filter the strong gusts that blow in during early spring. The shelter belt will in time be tall enough to carry the wind over its top so that wind continues to move some distance across the garden before it touches ground again. The filtered effect of the less densely planted windbreak slows the summer breeze as it moves through the garden, so that, hopefully, the delphiniums won't be flattened and the mood of the garden will be enhanced by soft breezes.

In small urban gardens, trees are used as wind filters simply because a true shelter belt would take up too much space. A few trees planted in a loose group in the direction of the prevailing wind will suffice to slow the breeze. Good air circulation is important for healthy plant growth, and this is especially important in the close environment of a town garden. Urban gardens are often fenced or walled, and these permanent structures alone do not provide a garden-friendly service since the wind will rise over the top and fall straight down the other side, creating a potentially damaging eddy. A few trees planted several feet away from the wall will, however, break the eddy and soften the blow of the wind as it falls on the plants below.

Shelters do provide an ornamental background, but since their primary purpose is functional you will naturally adopt a different set of selection and planting criteria from those you would use when making a purely aesthetic contribution to the garden picture.

Trees are also able to modify the climate within the garden. Apart from providing shade and shelter, they also help to keep ambient moisture levels up because the leafy canopy retards evaporation of water from the soil and also releases water into the atmosphere through transpiration (one of the processes of photosynthesis) which is one of the reasons why the decimation of the tropical rainforests threatens the survival of our species. On a more parochial level, leaf canopies cut airborne dust particles, keep the soil cool and, by exchanging oxygen and carbon dioxide, add to air purity in the garden environs.

Backgrounds

Background plantings should relate to the foreground planting, so if you are planning a low-key shrubbery, don't plant a collection of trees that have strong individual characters: it is better to stick to unassertive subjects that are in harmony with their surroundings. In my garden, which is made from a farm field, most of the plants in the remains of the old hedgerow have grown to mature trees, so the naturally occurring background is composed of hazelnuts, hollies, crab apples, hawthorn and field maple (*Acer campestre*). Consequently, the trees I have introduced include apples, more hazels, Italian alder, mulberry, quince and a small grove of *Prunus* 'Tai-Haku', the great white cherry, for a spectacular spring display of pink new leaves framing the clusters of white flowers, and an autumn show of reds and orange. My biggest mistake was a single poplar which looks as if it has grown taller than the garden is long and brings me to the next point.

Backgrounds can also be frames for a distant view, allowing you to borrow the landscape. This was a favourite trick of architects in Renaissance Italy, who adhered to the dictate proposed by Alberti in his *On the Art of Building in Ten Books* that a beautiful vista framed by the garden should be incorporated in every landscape design. But just as a painting and its frame must be sympathetic, so a 'garden' frame should relate to the view by repeating the dominant forms in that view: a vista of rugged mountain peaks should be set off by strong verticals and conical shapes, with low mounding shapes in the foreground to repeat the appearance of the landscape forms. Low, rolling hills and soft curves forming the view would find a sympathetic frame in a composition of rounded tree and shrub shapes, with clump-forming foliage perennials repeating the forms in the foreground. However, it is not enough simply to repeat the forms in the view – you must also keep them in proportion, which is why I should never have planted that poplar. It is a strident vertical out of scale with the size of the garden and the rounded forms of the old hedgerow trees and the other trees that have been planted.

The silvery nimbus of *Pyrus salicifolia* gives a soft focus background to the clearly defined geometry of a clipped box knot garden and the metal-frame arbour clothed in evergreen ivy *Hedera* 'Parsley Crested'.

Tonal contrasts give a garden vitality: the play of pale against dark, shadow against light can be achieved by using bright leaved plants to enhance the shadowy areas of garden, effectively adding visual depth to the layout.

Screening

Trees are also often used to provide screening, either to create seclusion within the garden or else to prevent the intrusion of unsightly elements from outside the garden boundaries. In a small garden, a screen will be linear, such as a row of evergreens or a line of pleached trees (usually beech or hornbeam), or will be a single specimen planted to block out an individual eyesore like a telephone pole. In a rural garden, there will be more room to plant small groups of trees, or even spinneys of one species. Start to do this, and you are following in the footsteps of Capability Brown who, if he couldn't demolish some offending element in the view such as a group of farm-worker's cottages, transplanted entire woodlands to obliterate it. Whatever the case, strive to keep the proportions and forms in harmony with the background and surroundings.

Shade is the other important contribution made by trees to the garden, and it provides more than just a place to sit out of the sun. The effect of contrasts in garden design can never be overstated, and the visual impact of light shade, deep shade and dappled shade can draw you through a garden as surely as a path of expensive stone paving.

The amount of shade you require will depend on the quantity of sun your garden receives and how you use your garden (including what you want to grow). During hot summer months the sun is high in the sky, almost directly overhead; during winter it moves across the sky at a lower angle. You may need the most shade during the middle part of the day through to evening on a terrace used for barbecues and evening meals, or you may require day-long shade over a specific part of the garden to protect moisture-loving plants.

The uniform pattern of four box-hedged squares provides a well-defined contrast to the informality of the surrounding planting scheme.

Selecting trees to provide shade requires you to consider their structure; whether they have large leaves, densely crowded branches and heavy crowns, or whether the leaves are small and loosely fill the fine branches on light, open crowns. The denser the shade the more cooling the effect will be for people to shelter beneath, but the less easy it will become to grow a wide range of plants below the tree.

Shade is an important consideration when siting evergreens; the dense shade they create will be permanent and so could have an adverse effect if, for instance, it is necessary to allow some warming sunlight to filter through to a group of plants during winter, or even to allow the weak but cheering rays of the winter sun to brighten a living room. To be perpetually subject to gloomy shadows is enervating, so it would be best to choose among the deciduous trees.

Hedges

Many trees are used to form hedges: this is their most potent structural use in landscape. Usually a formal hedge is a mono-type planting of one variety of tree, regularly pruned to encourage branching along the entire length of the trunk to create a dense barrier.

Most people prefer evergreen hedges, but too often they miss the opportunity to do something that will be of long-term bene-fit to the landscape and plant the ubiquitous Lawson cypress (x *Cupressus lawsoniana*) instead of the far superior yew (*Taxus baccata*) out of the misguided belief that yew is too slow-grow-ing. Actually, the reverse is true and the Lawson cypress is too fast-growing. A well-planted yew hedge, fed regularly with high nitrogen in early spring and general balanced fertilizer in the summer and watered regularly until established, will easily make 30-45cm (12-18 inches) growth in a year. A cypress will do more, of course, but is extremely vigorous, and could require two or three clippings each year to keep it in check. Who wants to spend all their time hedge-trimming?

Yew makes the finest ornamental evergreen hedge. Other popular evergreens are holly (golden-variegated holly hedges are quite spectacular), Portugese laurel (*Prunus lusitanicus*) and the larger-leafed *P. laurocerasus*; the last two make a rather gloomy contribution, in spite of their glossy, light-reflective leaves.

Hedges are also planted with deciduous trees, although the ever-popular beech (*Fagus sylvatica*) behaves like an evergreen, holding its caramel-brown withered leaves until the new foliage appears in the spring. Hornbeam (*Carpinus betulus*) is also widely used, and both trees are excellent when a high yet narrow hedge is required.

Tapestry hedges are a particularly attractive way to create informal or formal boundaries, and are planted using a mix of deciduous and evergreen trees; the old hedgerow bordering my garden is in effect a tapestry hedge, and against it the loose and extremely informal style of planting in the garden looks completely at ease.

Hedges can serve as screens, wind breaks, shelter belts or walls, dividing the garden into separate areas which can then be given individual treatments. Low-growing shrubby plants like dwarf box (*Buxus suffruticosa*), common thyme (*Thymus vulgaris*), certain small-leaf hollies and similar evergreens are used to make ground-covering linear patterns of tightly clipped hedging. Knot gardens are the most familiar device for taking advantage of these plants, but they can also be used to create ribbons of hedging like a green river to create movement through the landscape.

Hedge preparation and planting

Formal hedges are regularly clipped to maintain a uniform shape, while informal hedges where fruit and flowers are the

Frosted over or even covered in a blanket of snow, the woody structure of the shrubs remains visible throughout winter for true 'year-round interest'.

main attributes are not clipped other than to preserve an attractive shape. When planting a hedge, remember that while the plants need to be close together to form a dense barrier their natural growth is as tall-growing trees and while regular pruning and clipping perverts their innate tendency to develop large crowns, it does not disrupt their development of large root systems. If plants are put too closely together they will compete for food and water and some will inevitably die. There is no hard rule about spacing since it will depend on the tree you use, but 60-90cm (2-3ft) is not too much for a yew or hornbeam hedge. Hedging plants can be bought as containerized plants or else bare-root in bundles; deciduous hedging can be planted at any time of year, as can evergreens that are in containers, provided the weather permits (avoid periods of heavy frost or rain). Bare-root evergreens should be planted in the winter or early spring, as they are prone to desiccation and there is more moisture in the air at those times of year. Newly planted evergreens can be sprayed with an anti-dessicant to further assist their establish-ment. It is best to use young small plants rather than older and hence larger plants, since the youngsters will settle in more quickly and a young hedge if regularly fed will soon catch up in growth. However, if cost is not a factor but instant effects are and you plan on using older plants, you should also plan on keeping them well-watered throughout their first year. Prepare a trench at least 90cm (3ft) wide for large hedges, or 45cm (18in) wide for small and dwarf hedges. Double dig the trench, adding plenty of well-rotted manure or compost in the bottom spit and slow-release granular fertilizer in the backfill.

The most important thing is to keep a newly planted hedge free of weeds; this can be achieved by routine weeding, forking out perennial weeds and removing annual weeds before they seed; by spraying with contact and systemic weedkillers; or by mulching. The latter is the most effective measure, and a layer of 500g black polythene spread over the trench and buried along both edges to anchor it will not only keep weeds out, but will help to keep moisture in. The hedging is planted through

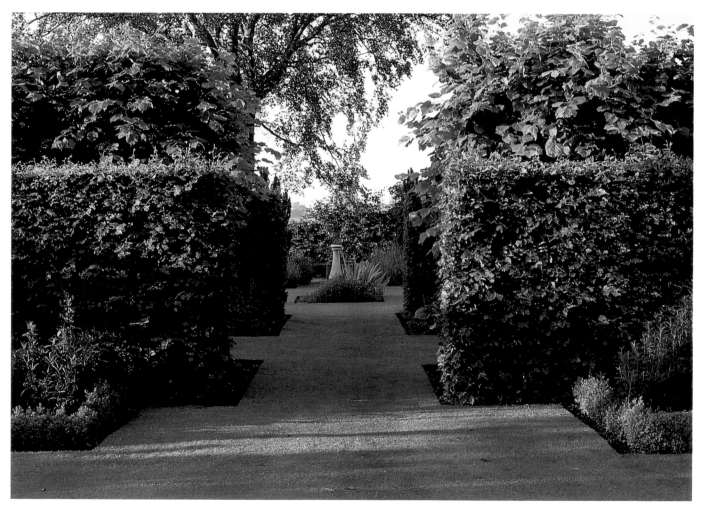

The view through a garden can be enhanced and given a feeling of greater depth by staggering the heights and textures of the hedges, as here where beech hedges alternate with a lime (linden) tree allée.

slits made in the polythene.

The first or formative pruning techniques vary according to the type of hedging used.

Deciduous, upright-growing plants must be encouraged to establish a framework of branches at, or near to, ground level. In the first year, cut top growth back to within 15cm (6in) of ground level. This removes the leader (main growing stem) and encourages many small branches to develop near the base of the plant. It also ensures that there is not too much top growth for the underdeveloped root system to support at the same time as the roots are striving to settle into the new site. In the spring of the year following planting, begin shaping the side growth by cutting back some of the new growth.

If, however, the hedge is destined to be a tall-growing windbreak the plants may be left unpruned until established, and then cut back to begin shaping by removing one-third of all the side growth.

Evergreens such as Lawson cypress should be staked in the first year with the main stem loosely tied to a bamboo cane to encourage the leader to grow upright. Any side growths that appear to be competitive with the leader should be cut back so that all growth is centred on the main upright stem.

Box and other small-leaved evergreens are shaped by cutting back side growths as necessary to achieve the desired width of hedge. Do not trim the tops until the desired height is reached. This should be done in mid to late summer.

After about two years, the hedge can be said to be established and a regime of regular clipping can be established to maintain the hedge shape. The top of the hedge can be trimmed as fancifully as you like – castellations, topiary shapes and so on – or simply shaped into a point or clipped flat. The contours, or batter, of the sides can be straight up and down, or tapered from narrow top to wide bottom, but the width must not be greater at the top than at the bottom; sunlight must reach all parts of the hedge evenly, which is why the batter is so important.

Old overgrown hedges of yew, beech, hawthorn, holly and hornbeam can usually be restored to a more suitable size by hard-pruning. The removal of over-long side growth lets light into the centre of the plant, which causes new healthy shoots to break from the old trunks. In the case of yew, begin by cutting back one side in the first year, then cut back the other side one or two years later, depending on how much growth the previously pruned side has made. After each pruning, feed and mulch the hedge.

Lavender hedges that have grown old and leggy may respond to hard-pruning done in the spring, but this is not guaranteed to be successful. Box is not renewable by hard-pruning, so it is better to start again with young plants.

Stilt hedges are created by keeping the trunks free of leafy branches from ground level to a desired height, usually 1.2-1.5m (4-5ft) and then the leader is cut to encourage the crown to develop a network of lateral branches which are then trained horizontally by tying them into a frame of wires or canes fixed to stakes. When the lateral growth is established the training framework can be removed and the crowns pruned hard each spring to encourage fresh leafy growth.

Stooling is a pruning technique in which all the top growth of shrub is cut back to a stump or to ground level to encourage the buds forming at the base of the plant to grow and replace the old wood which has been removed. The reason for stooling a plant is to make the most of its ornamental bark or foliage, since these qualities are superior on new growth. Trees and shrubs that can be stooled to enhance their seasonal effect include coloured-stem dogwoods, *Cornus sibirica*, *C. alba* and their cultivars; *Leycesteria formosana*; ornamental-stemmed species of *Rubus*; golden-leaved elder (*Sambucus racemosa* 'Plumosa Aurea'); purple-leaved elder (*S. r.* 'Purpurea'); African hemp (*Sparmannia africana*); yellow-leaved Indian bean (*Catalpa bignonioides* 'Aurea'); and variegated giant reed (*Arundo donax* var. *versicolor*).

Pollarding is like stooling on stilts, as it is the crown of the tree which is reduced to a frame of several stumps from which all the old stems are cut each spring. This encourages large leaves allowing the trees to provide good shade cover for paving and roadways in urban areas.

A stilt hedge is a popular visual device for enhancing perspective; here it effectively draws the eye through the garden to the stone arch and finally the countryside beyond. The trees are pollarded to create the effect.

Seeing green

When deciding upon a planting scheme there are various elements to consider but form will be the prime concern. Form refers to the outline of the whole plant – what it looks like in silhouette (*Fig. 1*) – and is allied to the idea of habit which refers to whether the plant is fastigiate, spreading, multi-stem or weeping (*Fig. 3*). Stem structure and to a lesser degree the shape of the leaves (*page 29*) help to determine the form. The style and manner in which plant forms are deployed throughout a scheme will determine the effect of the planting and define the atmosphere of the garden.

As a rule, upright vertical shapes are more emphatic than horizontal rounded shapes largely because the latter is the form most familiar to us being the one commonly encountered in nature. For this reason, designers rely on columnar forms to create eye-catching interludes in a garden plan. But for every exclamation mark in the garden, you will want to have rhythmical interludes or the effect becomes 'jumpy' and these are best achieved by a repetition of forms. Garden design is mostly about manipulating the senses to influence how we perceive our surroundings, and the repetition of plant forms creates a pattern of comfortable familiarity (particularly when assembled from friendly rounded shapes). However, repeated forms must be finely balanced by a variety of other forms to avoid evoking a feeling of monotony. In the photograph *(below left)*, a sequence of clipped box balls make an emphatic statement as they roll in formation across the lawn. The regimented formality of the glossy green spheres is saved from monotony by the surrounding informal masses of various plant forms and foliage: a backdrop of trailing curtains of golden hops (*Humulus lupulus* 'Aureus'), feathery fronds of male fern (*Dryopteris filix-mas*), sweet cicely (*Myrrhis odorata*) and alexanders (*Smyrnium perfoliatum*).

Similarly, but in different surroundings with different plants, the startling spikiness of a desert garden *(below right)* with linear shapes and strong verticals created by the upright cactus *Trichocereus pasacana* and the towering spikes of numerous yucca species, is relieved by a uniform scattering of spherical *Echinocactus grusonii*.

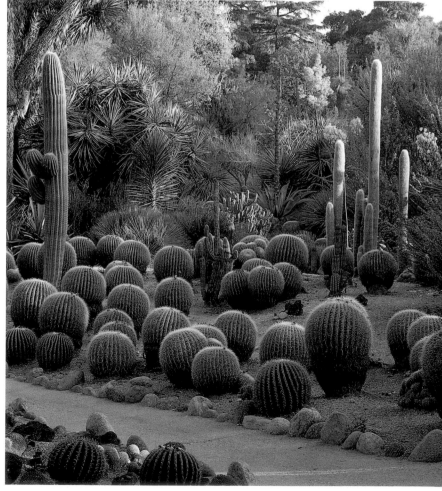

Rounded forms and strong verticals can be gained from many types of plants either naturally, as with the highly specialized leaf forms of cacti, or artificially, from clipped shrubs. Repetition of form creates a feeling of unity.

Fig.1 Tree Form

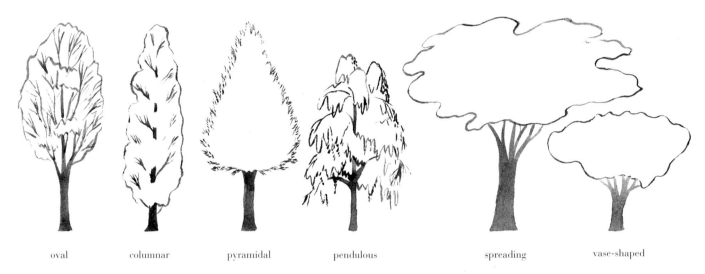

oval   columnar   pyramidal   pendulous   spreading   vase-shaped

Fig.2 Shrub Form

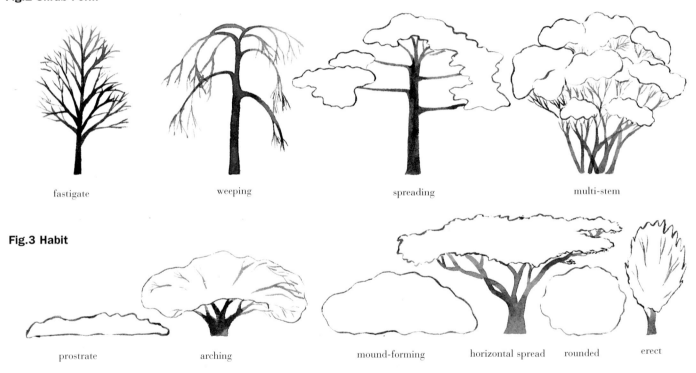

fastigate   weeping   spreading   multi-stem

Fig.3 Habit

prostrate   arching   mound-forming   horizontal spread   rounded   erect

Interestingly, because this particular cactus does not have leaves, its form depends entirely on the shape of its stem and is therefore totally natural, whereas the form of the box although naturally fairly rounded is enhanced by regular clipping. These particular topiary shapes are cut from the common box species, *Buxus sempervirens*, so that the shapes are rather unexpectedly large. We most often see clipped box balls created from the dwarf cultivar, 'Suffruticosa'.

Specimen trees

A specimen tree does not have to mean single tree, and when trees are to be planted as markers in the landscape – something that will attract attention to a vista or area of planting – few things can be more eye-catching than a multi-stemmed tree, or a group of three or five trees all of the same variety. Generally, trees treated in this way tend to be rather ordinary subjects, like birch trees, and it is

The strident colouring of *Acer* var. *heptalobum* 'Osakazuki' has the same visual impact as the breathtaking woody structure of a huge specimen of the pine, *Pseudotsuga menzieii*.

Trees with fine foliage, like *Acer palmatum* (*left*) and *Nyssa sylvatica* (*opposite*) make outstanding specimens which should be highlighted by sitting them to catch the light, or else positioned so that they appear silhouetted against a darker background. Other trees, however, can be exploited by emphasizing the interesting curves and angles of their trunks and branches, as with the gnarled trunk and spreading crown of the *Acer palmatum* var. *dissectum*, (*top*) or the unique configuration of habit and foliage in a specimen evergreen like *Pinus strobus* 'Pendula' (*above*).

by planting in this way that they become something special.

Single specimen trees are, however, a class apart: choice varieties or cultivars that are selected because of the unique contribution they make to the garden scheme. Most of the trees in my garden are common fruit trees. The apple orchard of heritage varieties interrupts one long axis, and the great white cherry grove makes an impact in spring and again in autumn, and in a way these features constitute specimen planting. *Liquidambar styraciflua* 'Worplesdon', one of only two specimen trees in the garden, is planted at a curve in the path and marks the transi-

tion between the ornamental and wilder parts of the garden. From late summer when the leaves begin to colour until the first hard frost, the tree is like a flaming beacon. At ten years old it is still making height, but will soon begin to compensate by increasing its girth, becoming an even more powerful magnet, pulling me spiritually and physically into the garden.

Scale remains an important consideration when selecting a specimen tree, because it would be a grave mistake to select a large tree for a small courtyard garden. Likewise, to set a small-growing specimen tree adrift in a vast country garden lawn would be unwise.

Shape is the other consideration. The shape of a tree planting refers to the overall outline of a group of plants composed from their individual forms. Tree forms are determined by the angle at which the branches are held away from the trunk: fastigiate or columnar forms occur because the angle between branch and trunk (the crotch) is narrow. and the lateral stems rising from the branches are also held at narrow angles causing the branches to be held upright or erect. The word 'fastigiate' signifies this form. Many tree species will have fastigiate varieties or cultivars: *Taxus baccata* 'Fastigiata' and *Betula pendula* 'Fastigiata' are commonly seen. while the evergreen Italian cypress (*Cupressus sempervirens*) is the most elegant of fastigiate trees.

Some trees will have branches held at angles near to 90°. which will give a graceful. broad. spreading form. like that of the magnificent cedar of Lebanon (*Cedrus libani*) while some will have much wider-angled crotches. giving the tree a pendulous effect: *Corylus avellana* 'Pendula' is the pendulous form of hazelnut. Rounded trees with regular outlines will have a much-branched crown and no central leader (main trunk).

Pyramidal trees (*pyramidalis* in botanical parlance) have a strong leader and are much wider branching at the base than near the growing tip at the end of the leader; liquidambar has this form. Vase-shaped trees have upward-sweeping branches, so the tree has an outline like an inverted triangle: *Prunus sargentii* is an example of this form. One of the best ways to acquire an understanding of form and habit is to study the naked silhouette of deciduous trees in the depth of winter, when the landscape is reduced to sharp contrasts of dark and light. The outline and structure of the trees will be immediately apparent. It will also be easier to observe the form of various evergreens when they stand out more clearly against their deciduous companions.

If you look at the natural landscape you will probably notice how the plant forms within it reflect the forms of the terrain: pyramidal conifers seem to repeat a horizon of mountain peaks; gentle rolling landscapes find their complement in the rounded forms of deciduous trees whose broad spreading crowns seem to follow the horizon line of open ground.

Shrubs

The next layer below the tree canopy is occupied by shrubs. While a tree is a woody perennial, deciduous or evergreen, that will grow to at least 6m (20ft) or more on a single stem, a shrub is defined as a woody perennial, deciduous or evergreen, that will reach a height of up to 6m (20ft) and has many stems.

Like trees, shrubs have form, but because of their shorter stature (and some are very low-growing indeed) they may be prostrate or creeping, trailing or mat-forming. Others will have branches that spread out horizontally, like *Viburnum plicatum* 'Mariesii', while others are erect, like *Viburnum* x *bodnantense* 'Dawn'. Fig. 2 (*page 22*) shows common shrub forms.

You begin to exercise your skill as a garden designer when you assemble trees and shrubs to form the permanent framework of the garden picture. Most typically they are combined in groups that depend upon contrasting forms for their interest. For exam-

Shrubs make a major contribution to the understorey planting either by unifying trees and lower level plantings of perennials and annuals or as single incidents in the landscape, like this thicket of *Rhus typhina* 'Lacinata'.

ple, if you have a fastigiate or erect form, a low-spreading form could be put at its base with a small rounded form to one side as a counterbalance. This grouping could then be used to establish the theme throughout the planting, and while the plants themselves might vary, their forms would not.

This theme could be used as an alternative to the formal clipped hedging described earlier, with ribbon plantings of erect and spreading shrubs forming a division of space within the garden, or forming its enclosing boundaries.

Perennials and ephemerals

Below and sometimes on a level with the shrub layer is the perennial layer, where herbaceous perennials, annuals and biennials serve as fill-ins to the composition. Often these are linking plants, bringing together separate areas of planting. One of the cleverest and most effective garden planting methods I know

begins by planting several trees in carefully prepared planting holes, at the proper distance to allow for shapely growth. The ground around the trees is heavily mulched to keep the soil surface weed-free. Once the trees are established, the shrubs are planted into carefully prepared planting holes and the soil is mulched and kept weed-free. When the shrubs are growing well – which they usually are by the following season – any turf remaining between the plants is removed, the ground is dug and manured, and perennial groundcovers are planted. Hostas and hellebores thrive in this regime, as would any other plant that appreciates the cool moist soil and semi-shaded conditions of a woodland garden.

Groundcovering plants create the final layer, and include many trailing plants and climbers that can look as effective carpeting the ground as they do draped on walls and fences. Groundcovers are also functional, helping to conserve soil moisture and suppress weeds.

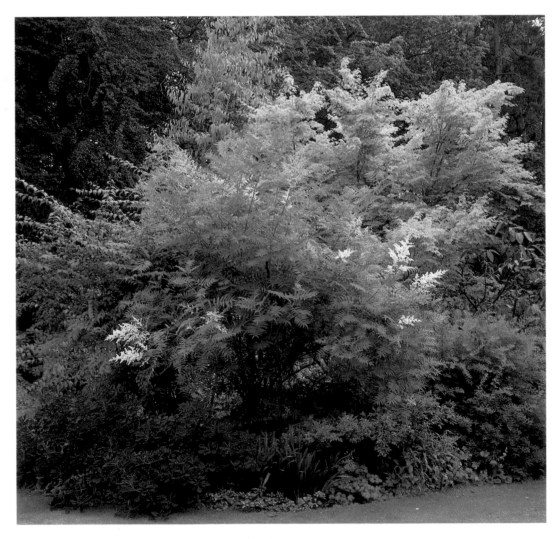

The light tones and soft textures make a cohesive group of *Eucalyptus glaucescens*, *Acer palmatum* 'Senkaki', *Sorbaria aitchisoni*, *Rosa nitida* and *Spiraea* 'Arguta' and one which stands out well against the evergreen planting behind.

The broad, coarsely textured leaves of hostas and hydrangeas combine with bold contrasts of dark and light between *Ophiopogon planiscapus* 'Nigricans' and pale-leaved perennials (*left*) to make a more visually demanding scene than the restful atmosphere created by the finely textured plants in the garden above, where the tints of green are virtually all the same tone. Contrasts give emphasis to planting schemes and features, like the boundary wall of the garden (*opposite*) which is clothed in *Euonymus* 'Silver Queen' and shod with *Dryopteris filix-mas* 'Cristata Martindale'.

Suiting the situation

Trees and shrubs are the largest group of ornamental plants, and when you sit down with a glossy gardening book it is all too easy to get sidetracked by a pretty leaf, interesting bark texture or the siren promise of glittering autumn fruit. The best way to determine your requirements is to assess what you need from the garden, and how that can best be achieved in the context of the site conditions within which you are working. You should never try to turn a dry sunny garden into a moist woodland, but trees and shrubs can create areas of cooling shade, and sculptural forms of specimen trees can be selected to add drama when viewed against the glittering sky. Grass turf is a foliage groundcover, but one which requires plenty of moisture to do well; if water shortages are a problem in your area, try gravel instead, and use hummock-forming grasses as ornamentals, combined with silver-leaved shrubs.

By adhering to a loose agenda of suiting plants to their envi-ronment you will find that the plants look 'right' together. By loose agenda, I mean one which permits, for example, the use of dry-shade lovers from those parts of the world which share similar minimum winter temperatures, rainfall patterns and elevations; a strict agenda could mean that you are limiting yourself to only those 'native plants' which occur naturally in your climate zone. There are too many wonderful plants to grow to be so narrow-minded.

Leaf form, texture and colour

The reason plants with similar horticultural requirements will appear cohesive is because their appearance will have adapted to accommodate conditions. For instance, plants from hot dry regions will have narrow or small and finely divided leaves to help the plant conserve water; in such areas there will be plenty of sun, so the leaves do not need a high chlorophyll content, and are often coloured grey to help reflect light and reduce surface

Fig.4 Leaf Shapes

ovate lanceolate elliptic linear obovate deltoid

pinnate palmate bipinnate compond palmate trifoliate

temperatures. Plants from hot dry countries also often have fuzzy or hairy surfaces, another feature to help cut water loss.

In the rainforest, light levels are low, so leaves must be large, and arranged along the stems as horizontally as possible in order to capture as much sunlight as they can; the shiny waxy surface helps to prevent the leaves losing too much moisture through evaporation in the high humid temperatures of the jungle. Similarly, the leaves of woodland shrubs and perennials from temperate zones are frequently broad, flat and held face to the light source to gather the maximum amount of sun and the plants benefit from the moisture levels provided by the sheltering leafy tree canopy overhead.

Cactus leaves are among the most specialized, with a solid structure designed to gather and hold as much water as possible during the occasional desert rains, and leaves often arranged in a pattern of concentric rings which channels the rainwater directly to the base of the plant and the root; the prickles and

thorns are there to discourage predators. There are hundreds of different leaf configurations, but some of the most commonly seen forms are shown in Fig. 4 (*page 29*).

Nature has also created some leaves with variegation, although this is generally a mutation caused by a virus, or else a genetic kink. The more variegated a leaf is the less chlorophyll it contains and the less able it will be to absorb sunlight, which is why variegated leaves often scorch in sunlight. Other leaves will have red or brown colouring, which may possibly serve as a deterrent, protecting the plant from foraging insects and herbivores. Other defence mechanisms include thorns on stems and prickly or hairy leaves that either make the plant unpleasant to chew or else act as micro-hypodermics to inject irritants and poisons when the plant is attacked. Other plants may have toxic roots or leaves. One of the main reasons it took the tomato and the potato such a long time to catch on in Europe was that people, not knowing how to handle the unfamiliar plant, ate the

Cacti, such as this *Azureocereus hartligianus* (*above*) or *Pachycereus pringlii* (*opposite*) offer spectacular foliage; although not frost hardy, if pot-grown they can be put out in the summer garden to add an invigorating contrast to the soft foliage of familiar perennials.

Seasonal colour provided by foliage is one of the gardener's greatest joys, and while some plants are known to colour well, the intensity and duration of the display is dependent on less predictable weather conditions which influence the plant's performance.

foliage as well as the fruit – with bitter consequences!

Leaves are coloured according to the levels they contain of certain pigments which are an important aid to photosynthesis. The main one, and most efficient for the photosynthetic process, is chlorophyll, and the greener the leaf the higher the chlorophyll content. Red and dark mahogany brown leaves contain a higher proportion of a vinous red pigment, anthocyanin. Carotene is an orange pigment and xanthrophyll pigments range from yellow to neutral. The levels of these pigments in a leaf determine whether it is acid green, butter yellow, blue-green, chocolate brown and so on.

Autumn colour is the result of a plant's response to seasonal changes. This can happen very suddenly or quite gradually depending on the plant and what the weather is like as the plant begins to shut down for winter, at which time it concentrates its

energy on food storage rather than production. The specimen *Liquidambar styraciflua* 'Worplesdon' in my garden colours slowly, turning at first a dirty green, but then the red pigments come to the fore as the chlorophyll-rich part of the leaf fades. By mid-autumn the whole tree is rich burgundy red, with hints of flame orange. This happens regardless of the weather. The other specimen tree, *Betula maximowicziana*, is entirely dependent on the weather for any autumn glory. In fact, I had begun to wonder why I had planted it at all, until one autumn when the days remained dry and sunny and the nights became very cold. The leaves continued food production in the daytime, but the transfer to storage was slowed by the cold night temperatures. The tree turned the most stunning and intense egg yolk yellow, and each large, heart-shaped leaf fluttered brilliantly against the blue sky. I had simply forgotten how perfect an autumn tree it

The larger the leaf the coarser the texture will appear. *Left*, the clearly defined medium-sized leaves of *Epimedium* x *perralchicum* present a more refined appearance than the robust oversize foliage of *Rodgersia podophylla* and *Lysichiton americanus*, *right*.

was, given the optimum autumn conditions for good colour-comprising dry, sunny days and cold nights. And when the leaves dropped, they did so all at the same time, leaving a pool of sunshine on the ground.

Perennial plants also have autumn colour attributes, but to a lesser extent than trees. Sometimes hostas can hold their foliage intact through a dry autumn and turn butter yellow. Ornamental grasses turn biscuit beige or tawny gold as the pigments fade. Some foliage perennials that have a reddish cast, for example bergenias and heuchera, will become redder as the weather gets colder. Gold variegations on evergreens like holly, elaeagnus and box seem to become richer in the winter, but that may be more to do with the fact that there is little competition from other plants, many of which will have retreated below ground, in the bright-colour stakes.

Foliage and planting design

In addition to the form and habit of a plant, the other physical characteristics which will influence how the plants are used in garden design are texture and colour.

Textures can be described as fine, medium or coarse, matt, glossy, heavy or light and combinations of these qualities will further define the plant's texture. For instance, a common cherry laurel with its broad shiny leaves held stiffly away from the stems could be described as coarse and glossy; rosemary would be seen as fine and matt. If a leaf is covered in fine hairs, it will absorb light and so have a softer look. Thus, these descriptive attributes are determined by the physical characteristics of the leaves, stems and bark, how they relate to one another, and how light is absorbed or reflected by their surfaces.

Top Santolina neapolitana 'Edward Bowles' has finely cut, dense silvery foliage which gives it a delicate 'soft focus' quality in contrast to the coarser appearance of the *Sedum spectabile* in the background. *Above* Fairly smooth broad flat leaves, like those of *Peltiphyllum*, will reflect light while deeply textured leaves like those of the chinese cabbage 'Nagaoke', *right*, absorb it.

As a general rule, the larger the leaf and heavier the branch the coarser the appearance of the plant. But loose, open foliage will also make the plant look coarse. Small-leaved plants, like box, that have dense foliage will appear softer.

The form of the individual leaves will also influence the appearance of the plant, with compound leaves appearing softer than large simple leaves. Just think of a maidenhair fern frond; what could be softer and finer than its complex leaves made of tiny individual leaflets on dark wiry stems? Conversely, a hart's tongue fern with its single, broad, flat leaf appears coarse by comparison.

In garden design, the textural qualities of foliage plants and their relationship in plant groupings should be carefully considered. Soft matt textures, like that of yew, beech, or hornbeam,

Top Edible plants. like the mustard greens 'Red Giant' and pak choi cabbage often have arresting foliage and can be used as filler plants in the garden.
Above Contrasts give emphasis: here rounded hosta leaves are set against the strap-like foliage of crocosmia and wands of willow gentian. *Right* Similarly.
the upright habit of the fern fronds is enhanced by the spread leaves of the rodgersia.

make the best backdrops for showing off other flower or foliage plants. because their dense shadowy quality makes a perfect low-key partner: glossy. coarse holly would be too assertive and distract attention from the foreground plantings. However. to emphasize a boundary. or to create an attention-getting device. holly would be hard to better.

Contrasts of texture. size and shape are what make plant groupings lively and interesting to look at: they hold our attention by the quality of the pattern they create. But a grouping must be executed thoughtfully: a jumble of many different plants will look just that. Simplicity is the key to successful planting.

Contrasts should never be played out simply as jarring juxtapositions: putting a spiky fastigiate tree with a low soft rounded shrub is too abrupt a transition. Add a loose open shape, however, and the composition is much more pleasing because it is easier on the eye.

Northern-hemisphere gardeners are used to soft even shapes and flowing lines, which is why, when viewing a tropical garden planted with spiky palms, bristling with cacti, padded out with succulents and glowing with glossy broad-leaved foliage plants in every shape and size, we find the whole scene quite spellbinding. It may, in part, be a gardener's version of 'the grass is always greener', but the theatrical effects of plants like this can be used to give drama to our tame temperate gardens. Not all gardeners have the wherewithal to grow true exotics – heated greenhouses do not come cheap. Some plants we use, however, like the giant *Gunnera manicata*, have exotic-looking leaves, as do the ferny fronds of the tree of heaven (*Ailanthus altissima*). Bamboo is exotic by nature, but hardy enough in most gardens to be used to good effect. When plants like this are employed, it should be done to make a point – to attract attention to a part of the garden – rather than deploying them wherever the oppor-

tunity presents itself. In the same way, focal points benefit from having a strongly patterned foliage plant at the epicentre. A clutch of sumach (*Rhus typhina*) planted against a light background, or on a high point where the bent and crooked branches and palm-like leaves will be silhouetted against the sky, makes good use of this plant's highly individual characteristics. One of the most beautiful trees is the variegated dogwood (*Cornus controversa* 'Variegata'), which has small leaves that are variegated creamy white with branches held in ascending tiers like a silvery pagoda. I have seen this tree planted at the foot of a gently rising slope in a woodland garden. Planted to be centre-stage as one descends the main axial path into the garden, its spreading branches reach out, drawing you ever further into the leafy shadows along the grassy ride leading through the garden. It is the most effective and dramatic visual statement, and sets the tone for the entire garden. From that moment you know that every plant will have been placed with a great deal of careful thought.

Above Some plants are outstanding simply because of their unfamiliar, hence exotic, appearance and colouring, like this English garden 'tropical border' planted with canna lilies, ricinus, jacaranda and a host of other half-hardy plants. *Opposite* A few plants have stand-alone elegance and, like the variegated dogwood *Cornus controversa* 'Variegata' illustrated here, should be given focal point status.

Colour

Colour is an emotive issue in more ways than just encouraging highly charged discussions between gardeners – 'I can't stand purple', 'One more white garden and I'll scream'. Colour influences our lives in so many ways. Grey skies are gloom-making; sunshine cheers. Pink calms, yet red is a signal to anger. And green cools and soothes the soul.

Monochromatic colour schemes are a popular device, as in the famous white garden at Sissinghurst or Hidcote's red borders. Green gardens are less common although in Japan, gardens which depend on a naturalistic use of foliage are central to the architectural content of temple enclosures. Even domestic gardens, in a land-poor country, are miniature representations of the natural woodland of mountain and valley. Moss gardens are an extreme example of a monochromatic foliage garden. The groundcover is a sheath of mosses and lichens, shaded by carefully pruned pines and clumps of bamboo; ornament is minimal and the interest is held entirely by the spirituality of the scene.

The Italian Renaissance garden is, perhaps, a more familiar monochromatic garden, where clipped hedges and carefully pruned trees serve to focus all our attention on the architecture of the villa, the statuary and the hard-landscaping features of the garden itself. As in a moss garden, few species are used. Usually there is box, clipped into tight low hedges or topiary; evergreen oak (*Quercus ilex*) is used along with bay (*Laurus nobilis*) and cypress (*Cupressus sempervirens*) to make background and major boundary hedges. Cypress and umbrella pines make pronounced vertical accents. The groundcovering plants are typically ivy and rough grass, but the turf is generally a tapestry of 'weeds' – plantains, prunella, thyme, ajuga, creeping mints and all sorts of little-leaved plants that we would be quite happy to cultivate in borders, but break our backs removing from the lawn. Highly formalized, architectural gardens in the Italianate style have an intellectual repose in the unfolding order and geometry of the landscape.

 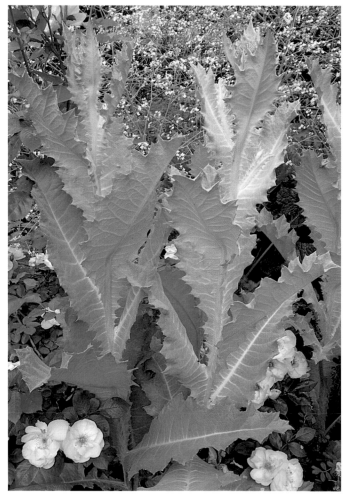

Monochromatic colour schemes are popular in gardens. *Left* White variegated hostas underpin white violas and tulips 'White Dream' and 'Maureen'. *Right* *Onopordum acanthium* is thrown into sharp relief by the filmy flowers of *Crambe cordifolia* and the rose 'Jacqueline Du Pré'.

Harmonies and contrasts can be developed out of a mono-chromatic scheme, because although a garden is green, there are many different tints of green, ranging from the silvery grey-green *Artemisia canescens* to the midnight green of *Ophiopogon planiscapsus* 'Nigrescens'. The colour wheel shown here is an indication of the range of colours available when planning a foliage garden.

A colour harmony occurs when adjacent colours in the colour wheel are used together. Thus, on the true colour wheel, where red, blue and yellow are the primary colours, the harmonies would be created by red, purple and blue; blue, green and yellow; red, orange and yellow; red, purple and orange and so on. Two colours would probably dominate while the third colour

Tints of green can be organized in a manner similar to the true colour wheel as there are blue-greens, yellow-greens and red-greens and corresponding hues in between. Just as the true colour wheel is the basis for flower planting schemes, so the 'green wheel' can be used to organize foliage, bark and berry for genuine 'year-round' colour in the garden. *Clockwise from top left corner*, the plants are: *Carya ovata* (butter yellow); *Helichrysum petiolare* 'Limelight' (silvery pale yellow); *Artemesia ludoviciana* 'Silver Queen' (silver grey); *Elymus magellanicus* (pale grey); *Hosta sieboldiana* var *elegans* (slate grey); *Eryngium bourgatii* 'Oxford Blue' (blue violet); *Ajuga reptans* 'Atropurpurea' (purple); *Ophiopogon planiscapus* 'Nigrescens' (black green); *Rodgersia podophylla* (brown); *Magnolia grandiflora* (dark green/khaki); *Gunnera manicata* (mid-green); *Lysimachia nummularia* 'Aurea' (acid yellow).

would be used to lift the scheme. This can be translated to the green colour wheel so that, for example, silver grey (*Stachys byzantina* 'Cotton Boll'), pale dove grey (*Lychnis coronaria* 'Alba') and silvery yellow (*Verbascum pulverulentum*) could be blended, or ruddy purple (*Vitis vinifera* 'Purpurea') with dark vinous green (*Salvia officinalis* 'Purpurea') and a touch of rusty brown (*Carex comans* Bronze Form). Working with tints of green is perhaps slightly more tricky as the colour bias is less obvious, but experience is a great teacher, and you will soon know how to see green in all its variety.

Colour contrasts rely on marrying complementary hues – colours that are opposite each other on the wheel. On a true wheel it would put purple and yellow, blue and orange and red and green together. On the green wheel, it would blend slate and pale grey with butter yellow or silver grey and yellow with dark purple.

Add in variegated plants or coloured stems and berries and the whole exercise takes on another dimension, yet these plants will have a predominant hue, be it yellow, white, red, blue or purple, and so can be associated with the appropriate segment of the green wheel.

The other way to use colour is to follow nature's lead. If you observe the changing seasons you will notice that each part of the year seems to carry its own colour scheme. Early spring is full of acid yellows, dark purples and vivid greens as the fresh young foliage unfurls. In the earliest part of the year a planting of dwarf conifer *Pinus mugo* 'Ophir', *Cornus stolonifera* 'Flaviramea', *Ajuga reptans* 'Catlin's Giant' and yellow- and green-variegated *Acorus gramineus* 'Ogon' would bring all these colours together. As summer moves in, the colours deepen, losing freshness until the end of the season brings in the fiery crimsons and honey and amber tones of ripening fields of grain. An unsprayed field of summer wheat sprinkled with crimson poppies is one of nature's most beautiful garments; the fine-leaved grass *Stipa tenuissima* fades to silky beige and planted with the yellow-daisy-flowered *Anthemis tinctoria* 'E.C. Buxton' would

Left Many yellow-leaved plants scorch in sunlight; the grass *Milium effusum* 'Aureum', seen here with *Hosta fortunei* var *albopicta* and the orange-flowered hybrid of *Trollius chinensis* will brighten a semi-shaded corner. *Right* Sunlight deepens the red colouring of the ornamental lettuce 'Petite Rouge'.

Contrasting colour schemes are notoriously tricky, evoking strong prejudices in the eye of the beholder. Particularly sensitive is the use of magenta red and saturated orange, as here in the cabbage 'Christmas Mix' planted with pumpkin coloured *Calendula* 'Orange King'.

recall this summer picture. Winter is monotone-time, when charcoal-dark branches are silhouetted against grey skies and evergreen shrubs and trees dominate the garden. A simple statement, like a well-branched specimen of *Betula nigra* 'Heritage', with its characteristic white bark lightly flushed with buff-apricot tints, silhouetted against the dark mass of a tight-clipped yew hedge, best captures winter's essence.

Just as the form and textures of a foliage plant can be used to manipulate our experience of the landscape, so can the way we use colour influence how we perceive a garden. There are certain characteristics of colour that can be used to set a mood, visually alter the perspective, or capture the attention. In the context of planting a foliage garden, it is well to remember that turgid, muddy colours can be fairly oppressive and so should be used sparingly, possibly as accents to brighter schemes. By using a predominance of grey or silver plants you can attempt to re-create a corner of the Mediterranean, but remember that in

sunny regions the soft foliage colours are set off by vivid flowers. In western gardens, a solidly emerald green garden modelled on a Japanese woodland will benefit by having touches of white, cream and ivory introduced in leaf variegations and flower colour.

Design alternatives

There are many ways to approach the design of a garden that relies heavily on foliage rather than flowers. If all the chat about colour, scale and form is too dry for your tastes, it might be more fun to choose an esoteric theme and collect the plants around that idea. One of England's greatest plantsmen, E. A. Bowles, had at his garden at Myddleton House a corner devoted to botanical oddities which he dubbed 'the lunatic asylum'. A friend of mine is developing a 'torture corner' devoted to plants with naturally twisted, gnarled or faciated (flattened) stems,

Santolina 'Lemon Queen', rosemary, box and artemisia are used to form the interlaced threads of a herbal knot, a device
that is one of the oldest uses of foliage plants in garden design: the woven effect is achieved by clipping the hedge
to differing heights.

grotesque thorns or hideous smells – not a part of the garden in which to linger. Brown-leaved plants would offer plenty of scope, from the splendid *Macleaya cordata* which can reach towering heights up to 2.4m (8ft), to the little ground-covering *Geranium sessiliflorum novae-zelandiae* 'Nigricans'. Macleaya is one of the best herbaceous perennials for foliage display. The leaves are glaucous grey touched with copper and the flower plumes are soft buff pink. It is quite invasive: once you have it you always will, and it runs around on its widely travelling roots. However, it is easy to pull up where it is not wanted and should be in every foliage garden worthy of the name.

Geranium sessiliflorum novae-zelandiae 'Nigricans' is another easy mover, and one of the best for brown foliage. The flowers are like little white stars and the whole thing is perfectly sweet. There are many hardy geraniums that have good foliage and are worth collecting. I would start with *Geranium robertianum*, the common herb robert of hedgerows and old herbals. The leaves are deeply cut and so have a light lacy appearance, and as the season advances towards autumn, the emerald green colouring turns deep ruby-red. They have a pungent resinous scent and all summer the plants are covered in little pink star-like flowers. There is a white-flowered cultivar 'Album', which is even more desirable. The plant throws its stems about, weaving in and out

of neighbouring plants. It is a freely self-seeding annual. *G. macrorrhizum* 'Ingwersen's Variety' has a similar resinous scent, but the leaves are rounded and have a slightly felted surface, and colour well in autumn. Used in mass plantings as groundcover beneath a stilt-hedge it makes an impressive sight. *G. renardii* is not particularly scented, but the leaves are soft grey-green and the plant shapes up into a pleasing mound that is covered in small white flowers in summer.

And if that's not enough, there are all the scented pelargoniums, tender relatives of the hardy clan, but with leaves that you select first for their scent and second for their interesting appearance. One of the most highly perfumed, and a favourite with Victorian conservatory gardeners, is 'Mabel Grey'. The leaves have the strongest citrus scent and the stiff, serrated leaves look like doll-size fans. 'Chocolate Peppermint' is deeply lobed, has a felted surface and the centre of each leaf is marked with a deep maroon 'chocolate' blotch. 'Acushla' has thumbnail-sized pearly green foliage strongly smelling of apples and incense; 'Odoratissimum' has a sandalwood and orange perfume and *Pelargonium crispum* 'Variegatum' has tiny ruffled leaves splashed with cream and scented of peppermint. There are more, so you could become obsessive, which I have. Because they are not hardy, my scented geraniums are housed in pots which stand

The lemon balm, *Melissa officinalis* 'Aurea', is variegated with splashes of bright yellow, particularly useful for lifting a dark corner.

out on the terrace during the summer. There, amidst the orange, lemon and olive trees which are also pot-grown, they bask in whatever sun comes our way, trying – and usually succeeding – to remind me of favourite Tuscan gardens. For winter, they are moved to the greenhouse and there kept frost-free, and when spring rolls around, the plants are repotted or given fresh compost and cut back to encourage a lush new growth of scented leaves. Their curious textures, odd shapes and attractive markings invite you to touch the leaves, and so release the scent.

Herb gardens

Scented foliage plants are varied and beautiful, and herb gardens are in essence foliage gardens. Try to look beyond their use as a flavouring or remedy and regard the plants as ornamental shrubs, herbaceous perennials, annuals or whatever. Study their form, habit and the textures and colours of individual leaves and you will see the potential for taking the herbs into the ornamental garden.

Few herb gardens are without lavender, and with good reason. Every part of the plant has the characteristic resinous sweet perfume. Lavender flowers come in white and shades of purple and pink to rose: cultivars from New Zealand like the pink-flowered *Lavandula* 'Marshwood' and dark red-purple *L*. 'Helmsdale' are pungently scented introductions. The foliage is typically lin-

ear and felt-soft in varying shades of grey; *L*. 'Sawyers' has wider and more silvery grey leaves than some of the new cultivars; the species *L. lanata* has particularly soft woolly leaves and *L. canariensis* and *L. dentata* are distinctly serrate.

Fine-textured and tall-growing fennel (*Foeniculum vulgare*) is especially beautiful as a fill-in plant among roses and delphiniums; the bronze-leaved fennel (*F. v. purpureum*) is so often seen in this context that it is easy to forget about the clear colouring of common green fennel. It is perennial but will also seed around freely. Dill (*Anethum graveolens*) is another feathery textured herb, but it grows to only about 45cm (18 inches) so should be saved for use among shorter growing annuals; I like it with the golden-stiped grass *Molinia caerulea caerulea* 'Variegata' and lady's mantle (*Alchemilla mollis*). Lemon balm (*Melissa officinalis*) is a rapid groundcoverer, scented highly of citrus; the cultivar 'All Gold' has pure yellow leaves and should be shaded from the midday sun since it will scorch.

The fern-like foliage of sweet cicely (*Myrrhis odorata*) gives the herb a fine texture. It is clear green, tall-growing and makes a good filler plant with herbaceous flowers.

Several perennial herbs are excellent architectural plants – ones that have strong and determined outlines that can be used as focal points in the garden. Foremost is doubtless the cardoon

Cynara cardunculus. It looks very like a globe artichoke, but the cardoon's huge leaves are more deeply lobed and each lobe more finely laciniated, and more silvery grey. It begins to push through the ground in early spring, and that is when it can be lifted, divided (it is easily propagated by offsets) and replanted, which should be done regularly since young plants provide better foliage. It will soon make a vast clump of arching grey leaves up to 1.2m (4ft) across, eventually throwing up an erect, thistle-headed flower. This should be removed as the foliage will begin to deteriorate if the cardoon is allowed to flower; cut the stem as near to the base of the plant as possible.

The compound leaves of the tall-growing lovage (*Levisticum officinale*) are dark green, glossy and quite coarse in appearance. Angelica (*Angelica archangelica*) has similar textures and gloss but the leaves are paler green and slightly larger than lovage. The stems and leaves of *A. gigas* are tinged with port-purple.

Laurus nobilis the ever popular bay tree, is often used to make ornamental standards and geometric topiary since the stiff green leaves hold the shape well. The green is rather a dull mid-tone, so if you want the formal shaping but in a bolder colour, try the cultivar *L. n.* 'Aurea', which has good golden-green leaves. They do scorch in full sun so the plant needs to be in a spot that is semi-shaded when the sun is at its height; the white variegation of 'Morroway Silver' makes the foliage look as though it has been sprayed with bleach.

Variegation

Variegation holds particular fascination for some plant collectors as well as for designers – a splash of bright yellow in a dark corner is a welcome sight. But to my eye – and all these considerations are highly personal anyway – variegation in moderation is best. It is easy to overdo, since the very nature of variegation removes some of the structural definition of a plant and thus if every plant used in a scheme were to be variegated the effect

could be nothing more than a fuzzy confusion of blotched and spattered leaves. Used with discretion, however, variegation can lift a planting scheme from the ordinary to the exceptional.

I like to see variegation at ground level because then the leaves become part of a tapestry covering the soil. Lamiums provide some of the finest bright colourings for moist soils in semi-shade. *Lamium galeobdolon* 'Hermann's Pride' has bright silver leaves netted with green veining; *L. g.* 'Silberteppich' ('Silver Carpet') is more purely silver-leaved. *L. maculatum* 'White Nancy' has white flowers and silver leaves while the cultivar *L. m.* 'Aureum' has bright budgerigar-yellow foliage with a silver flash down the midrib vein; it looks spectacular used with Bowles' golden grass (*Carex elata* 'Aurea')and other plants whose foliage tends towards yellow/green. Pulmonarias are good groundcovers in moisture-retentive soil in part shade; the leaf shapes range from shapely ovals to narrow tapering as seen in the fine cultivar *Pulmonaria longifolia* 'Bertram Anderson'. Variegation usually appears as silver blotching and spotting, but *P. rubra* 'David Ward' has soft grey-green leaves edged with cream.

Vinca major 'Variegata' always catches my eye, with the bold yellow and green splashes covering the glossy oval leaves. It spreads rapidly, rooting wherever it touches. *V. minor* 'Argenteovariegata' has faint white edging and splashes at the tips of the leaves, as does *Pachysandra terminalis* 'Variegata', another vigorous groundcover for semi- or full shade.

The rounded silvery leaves of *Saxifraga stolonifera* are covered in tiny hairs, and are tinged with the ruddy red colouring of the creeping stolons by which the plant will colonize moist, shady spots in the garden. In summer tall-growing flower stems up to 45cm (18in) tall shoot skywards, bearing dangling white moth-like flowers; a stunning plant for gardens, hardy to zone 6, but usually seen on the kitchen windowsill. Do yourself a favour and move it to the garden if you can.

The sagittate leaves of *Arum italicum italicum* 'Marmoratum'

Opposite Some variegated plants carry their colouring along the edges of the leaves like *Phlox paniculata* 'Norah Leigh' and spear-leafed *Sisyrinchium striatum*. Variegation permits some playful juxtapositions in a planting scheme, as with this cheerful display of the variegated *Euonymus* 'Emerald Gaiety' partnered with brightly coloured *Ribes sanguineum* 'Brocklebankii' (*above*).

Many good foliage plants have prettily tinted berries and should be included in a planting scheme for the contribution they make to late season colour: *left* is the yellow fruit of *Ilex aquifolium* 'Bacciflava'; *right* the rosy berries of *Sorbus* 'Kirsten Pink'; and *opposite*, the familiar crimson fruit of *Cotoneaster marquandii*.

are rich glossy green with the network of veins boldly picked out in silvery cream. From the early spring to midsummer the leaves look terrific, especially when used to make groundcovering clumps with hosta and hellebore. When the leaves have fallen away, the bold spikes of bright red berries poking through the mulch really do cheer a drab scene.

There are many variegated trees, but if you are planning on planting one, go for the best. Apart from the dogwood described earlier, the creamy variegated oak *Quercus cerris* 'Argenteovariegata' is a stunner.

Berries

After foliage and bark, berries are the remaining attribute that can increase a plant's worth in the garden, brightening up the dull parts of the year with vivid tints of red, yellow and orange, sapphire blue and ebony black. But berry colour is as transient as that of the flowers that precede it, and there are times when it will only last as long as it takes a flock of birds to strip the shrub of its jewels. Nature-lovers will, therefore, find selecting shrubs for berried treasure doubly rewarding, since they will be stocking the food cupboard for local fauna.

Holly and cotoneaster are probably the most widely known and widely grown berry shrubs, but pyracantha (firethorn) and snowberry are also hugely popular. Hot-coloured berries are the speciality of *Pyracantha coccinea*, and follow on from the sweet-scented clusters of tiny white flowers that shroud the plant in spring. Pyracanthas are frequently trained as wall shrubs and can be pruned to achieve ornamental latticework effects. *P. rogersiana*, *P.* 'Orange Glow' and the upright-growing *P. coccinea* 'Lalandei' have burnt-orange berries, and the former has a yellow-berried form, *P. rogersiana f. flava*. Pyracantha will grow anywhere and most are hardy to -15°C (5°F). However, for orange berries the sea buckthorn *Hippophae rhamnoides* is hard to better, although to grow it you need poor soil and a sunny spot. It grows naturally in coastal dunes and sandy soils of dry river beds from England to northwest China and its sturdy rounded shape, growing up to 10m (30 ft), can withstand strong winds, with or without salt. The stiff, narrow foliage is silvery grey-green and the whole plant has a wiry rugged look. The little spring flowers are followed by rusty orange berries that hug the stems along their length – provided you have planted both male and female.

The snowberry (*Symphoricarpos albus*) makes a small mounding shrub up to 1.2m (4ft). The arching stems carry pale pink flowers in spring which then form the clusters of pearly white berries that dangle among the tangled brown stems. It is a suckering, rather uninteresting shrub for most of the year, quite hardy and needs moist soil. It has a cousin, *S.* x *chenaultii*, that

has rosy pink berries and *S.* x *doorenbosii* 'Mother of Pearl' has berries streaked and splashed with cream, pink and rose.

The bamboo *Nandina domestica* is good value all year round, with the leaves changing from pinkish-brown juvenile colouring through dark green and finally to a rich purplish sepia in autumn, studded with clusters of glistening ruby-red fruit. When grown well it makes a spectacular low hedge. Bright red berries are an occasional feature of the elderberry *Sambucus racemosa* 'Tenuifolia'; it makes a low mounding shrub with a filmy appearance from the extremely narrow leaves which are tinged with purple when young.

Blue berries are attention-getters and the bluest is the sapphire berry (*Symplocos paniculata*). The deciduous leaves are heavily textured, glossy green ovals and the flowers appear like fuzzy white snowballs followed by the shining blue berries. This loose-growing shrub needs acid soil in sun or shade and will grow to 4.5m (15ft), so use it for boundary planting. Some viburnums have bright grapey-blue berries; *V. davidii* is especially good, with berry clusters held above the attractive evergreen foliage. *Drimys lanceolata* is a winter-flowering evergreen that has narrow tapering leaves and glittering little black fruit: the leaves and bark are scented of cinnamon and the flowers have a similar spiciness that warms the winter breeze. *Cornus sanguinea* has brick-red autumn leaves and clusters of shiny blueberry-black fruit.

Mahonias have holly-like compound leaves, and the racemes of sweet-scented flowers, reminiscent of lily-of-the-valley, are followed by sprays of bloomy blue fruit. The holly grape (*Mahonia aquifolium*) has good autumn colour, with the leaves becoming flushed with coppery purple, and the blue-black fruit makes delicious jelly that has an invigorating tanginess.

Rosehips are famously useful for jelly-making and have traditionally been used to make a health-giving syrup as they contain a large amount of vitamin C. The most lusciously hipped rose is the *R. rugosa* cultivar 'Scabrosa'. The foliage has the rugged texture and rich autumn gold colouring of other rugosas, and the flowers appear over an incredibly long season. A hedge of this rose is dazzling clothed in autumn colours with the cherry-pink flowers and huge crab apple-sized crimson hips all vying for attention together. It will sucker and spread easily, and can be sheared back in the late winter or early spring to ready it for the next extravaganza. *R. nutkana* 'Plena' is a vigorous, upright-growing rose; in autumn the current season's growth and the abundant clusters of little round hips take on a rich colour so that the plant appears to have dipped upside-down in red paint.

Tassels

Tassels are another aspect of plant interest that is worth mentioning. The branches of the hazelnut trees in the old boundary hedge that is part of my garden are adorned with buttery-yellow tassels in late winter to early spring and have spread themselves among the shiny

Flowers fade to berries and seedheads, which are the main reproductive part of a plant: like the seeds of *Hordeum jubatum*, *left*, and *Pulsatilla vulgaris*, *right*, they can also be curiously attractive.

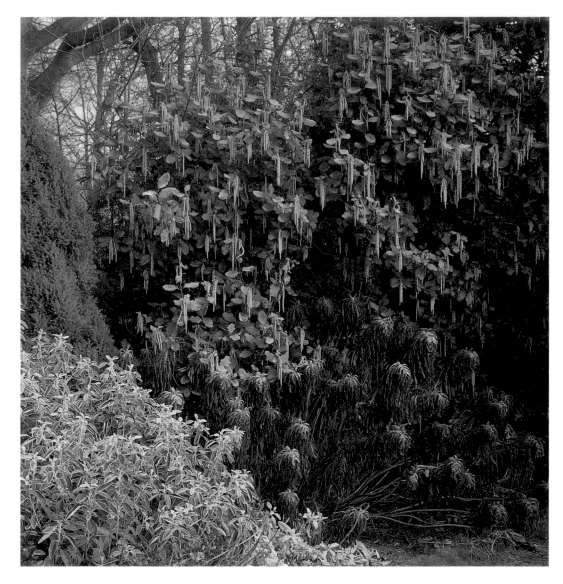

Tassels and catkins are underappreciated, yet their languorous habit and the way they catch the weak light in autumn or spring can bring a dull planting scheme to life.

thickets of emerald-green holly. A few scarlet berries still dot the holly trees at this time and the picture could not be prettier.

The common hazelnut (*Corylus avellana*) is tasselled, and there is also *C. a.* 'Contorta' which has crazily twisted stems and splendid clusters of soft white tassels: it is hard to look at this tree with any degree of comfort in summer since the leaves are all scrunched and wrinkled too, but winter nakedness and maturity improve it no end.

Itea ilicifolia is an evergreen that carries its flowers at the end of summer. They are sweetly scented and carried in tiny whorls around the long dangling tassels. It does best against a warm wall. *Garrya elliptica* is hardy but still needs full sun and shelter in winter to protect its winter-flowering tassels and leathery evergreen foliage from frost damage. When well grown it looks

most handsome, with the silvery felting on the undersides of the leaves setting off the pale green catkins to perfection. The cultivar *G. a.* 'James Roof' produces especially fine catkins as long as 30cm (12in) in good conditions.

Catkins are the main feature of the willow tribe, and one of the most pleasing is *Salix lanata*, which has round, heavily felted grey leaves that are held in tight bunches close to the stiff dark stems. The catkins are short stubby little caterpillars held upright like candles in silver sconces. *S. magnifica* is altogether more spectacular, making a deciduous shrub up to 6m (20ft) with leathery green oval leaves and female catkins up to 30cm (12in) long. The male catkins, held upright from the sinuous spreading branches, are half that length and tinged with red at the tips when young.

THE GARDENS

The ideal way to learn about garden design and planting is to look at how other people have approached the subject, and this can best be achieved by visiting gardens in your area, noting the plants that particularly interest you and talking to the gardeners. Not only will you be able to learn from their successes, you will also be able to learn from their failures!

The ten gardens on these pages make particularly good use of foliage, and demonstrate the points I have made in earlier sections about borrowing from nature to create gardens that are in harmony with their surroundings. The plans which accompany them are meant as rough guides to the planting schemes; they are not 'follow-me-or-fail' recipes. Instead, allow them to encourage you to investigate the many different species and cultivars within a genus.

Look and learn. Take in the broad garden picture, then narrow your focus down to the details of plant groupings, individual plants, and finally the plant structure of the leaves, bark and berries.

A garden appears to be painted in monochrome across winter's broad canvas, but the glitter of iced branches and frosted forms of evergreens and bare-stemmed deciduous shrubs emphasize the three-dimensional nature of a garden.

A winter garden

At Wollerton Old Hall, Lesley Jenkins has used foliage plants to provide interest in the garden throughout the year as well as to give the design structure. Beech hedges divide the space into distinct areas, the warm caramel brown colour of the spent foliage providing a mid-tone to the dark inky greens of topiary yew and glossy emerald of clipped box edgings. These three shrubs are widely used as structural plants.

Common European beech (*Fagus sylvatica*) is a robust plant that when left to its own devices makes a graceful large tree, but it is also amenable to a yearly clipping to make a fine decorative hedge. Although deciduous, the leaves do cling to the branches and only drop when the new foliage begins to appear in the spring, so a beech hedge has a quasi-evergreen quality and for some gardens this can be an advantage – as in this garden, where the ribbons of golden brown tie the various units together. However, I find that the brown leaves begin to look a bit tired by the end of winter and prefer hornbeam (*Carpinus betulus*) for this type of hedging. It drops its leaves in autumn, but a mature hedge provides a dense thicket of wiry branches. The juvenile foliage is acid green and has a pleasing cor-

Above Plants used to create a parterre similar to the one at Wollerton Old Hall in Shropshire are: I Clipped box balls; II Box hedge; III *Thymus pseudolanuginosus*; IV *Ilex aquifolium* 'Silver Queen'; V *Viola* 'Boughton Blue'; VI *Alchemilla mollis*; VII *Saxifraga* 'London Pride'; VIII Turf; IX Clipped yew cones; X Beech hedge; XI *Acaena saccaticupula* 'Blue Haze'; *Left* In summer the topiary shapes bring focus to the flower-filled enclosed garden. But it is the winter frost that enhances the solid evergreen forms, bringing them a sculptural quality that remains even under a thick blanket of snow.

rugated texture adding further interest as if in compensation for its winter nakedness.

The other beech which is occasionally used for hedging is *Fagus sylvatica purpurea*, the copper or purple beech, but a little of this colouring goes a long way, and a purple hedge used throughout a garden could be overwhelming.

In the parterre the beech hedge picks up the colour of the herringbone brick paving so that the floor and 'walls' of the garden room are unified by colour. At the centre a strong vertical accent is given by the lollipop standard of a clipped variegated holly, *Ilex aquifolium* 'Silver Queen', which in spite of its name is male (no

berries) and has leaves edged with creamy yellow. This holly sometimes throws out branches on which the leaves are pure glistening yellow. *I. a.* 'Golden Milkboy' (male) has its variegation in reverse with the gold splash at the centre of the leaf. *I. a.* 'Ferox Argentea' is the creamy yellow variegated hedgehog holly with spines along the upper surface of the leaf, giving a shrub a curious 'woolly' appearance when viewed from a distance. In England, where holly is native, it is regarded as 100 per cent hardy, but a severely cold winter can denude a tree. Thus, if your garden is in a region where winters are profoundly and prolongedly freezing, growing a holly as a containerized ornamental is an option worth considering, since it can be moved to shelter before winter sets in. Any of the clones from *I.* x *meserveae*, for example, *I. m.* 'Blue Angel' *and* I. m. 'Goliath', are very hardy and will keep their glossy green leaves throughout the coldest winter.

However, if you want to grow holly and won't mind the loss of leaves, go for the deciduous holly *Ilex verticilliata*, which has ruby-red berries glittering along naked branches throughout the winter; *I. v. aurantiaca* has orange berries and is hardy enough for continental winters.

While we're thinking of hardiness, *Ilex crenata* offers cold-climate gardeners a selection of small-leaved varieties that are good

A late summer border

Alan Gray's planting of a late-summer border at the Old Vicarage in east Norfolk makes the utmost use of clump-forming grasses such as pennisetum, miscanthus and pampas to create a leafy matrix for a limited palette of late-summer flowering perennials. Where most flower-dependent borders would have been cut down and tidied up before winter the grasses remain, along with some of the stiffer-stemmed perennials, to prolong the display in this part of the large formal gardens. So successful is this scheme that the border retains its beauty until the grasses are cut down the following spring, thus doubling its function by becoming a winter border as well.

At that time of year the grasses have faded to a soft biscuit beige, and combine well with ghostly silver shrubs like artemisia and lavender. The surviving branches of *Aster lateriflorus* form well-defined masses, as do clumps of dried flower stems from the various sedums. Among the billowing grasses, the upright sword-like leaves of *Phormium tenax* 'Purpureum' create a strong visual rhythm.

Earlier in the year the green grasses make a fine foil for the shocking pinks and purples of neighbouring flowering plants: in the background there are fronds of dark purple buddleia, *Buddleja davidii* 'Black Knight', complemented by bright yellow broom *Genista lydia*: in the middleground there are roses, *Anemone japonica*, *Fuchsia magellanica* var. *gracilis* 'Tricolor' and a number of Michaelmas daisies; the foreground is composed of sedums including *Sedum* 'Ruby Glow' and *S.* 'Vera Jameson', flushed deep cherry pink. *Schizostylis coccinea* scatters its cochineal-coloured flowers amidst the silvers and rusts of its companions, which include *Artemisia ludoviciana* 'Silver Queen', *A.* 'Powis Castle' and patches of felted grey lamb's ears (*Stachys byzantina*). The warm pinks and violets of these flower colours are concentrated in the purple-bronze foliage of the phormium and *Heuchera* 'Palace Purple', and also help to draw attention to the delicate colouring of the grass flowers.

Pennisetum alopecuroides is probably the most beautiful of the fountain grasses; the cascading leaves make a fine soft mound, above which the dusty pink flowers dangle like furry caterpillars caught on a line. *P. a.* 'Hameln' is a lower-growing variety and *P. villosum* has the longest bristles for an even softer effect in the border. The flower plumes of the *Miscanthus* cultivars have a similar rosy glow, but their reflective texture gives them a silken shimmer. Grasses are monocots, fertilized by

This splendid border has everything you could ask for: colour, texture, movement, myriad contrasts in height, depth of tone and all is provided by the foundation of mixed grasses and strong foliage plants artfully composed with carefully blended flower colour.

Scale is an important consideration when planting containers and, in general, the bigger the better as a large pot or huge basket such as this allows for a wider range of more dramatic plants to be grown to make real impact.

P. madagascariensis commonly called variegated mintleaf takes the high point in the composition, with the broad felted leaves of *P. fruticosus, P. argentatus* and dark-tinted *P. oertendahlii* below. To contrast with the rounded shapes of this foliage, *Senecio kleinia* is used for its succulent steel-blue fingers.

A small, shallow lead trough is planted for high contrast, with the rosette-forming succulent *Echeveria glauca* played off against the strappy leaves of the hardy perennial black 'grass' *Ophiopogon planiscapus* 'Nigrescens'. High tonal contrasts feature again in the planting of the oak-leaved peppermint-scented *Pelargonium* 'Chocolate Peppermint' with its purple black-centred furry leaves supporting the soft green and mottled cream *Fuchsia magellanica* var. *gracilis* 'Variegata'. The leaves and stems of the background plant, *Fuchsia* 'Gartenmeister Bonstedt', repeat the inky colour of the peppermint geranium.

Butter-yellow variegations mottle the huge round leaves of the perennial *Petasites japonicus* var. *giganteus* 'Variegatus' which,

with a white-edged hosta, set the colour themes of a wall-mounted basket. The yellow is repeated in the delicate crown of daisy flowers of *Argyranthemum* 'Jamaica Primrose' and the grassy leaves of gold-striped *Hakonechloa macra* 'Alboaurea'; the trailing variegated mintleaf adds to the white variegations and purple-leaved *P. oertendahlii* and more of the dark-hearted 'Chocolate Peppermint' pelargonium give tonal depth.

The plantings in each of the previously described containers are fairly complex, and their impact is heightened by the unifying repetition of certain plants. Yet there are also simple schemes that make use of only two plants, one for flower, the other for foliage, partnered for complementary effects, such as the lime-green trailing *Helichrysum petiolare* 'Limelight' and burnt orange-flowers of *Begonia sutherlandii*.

One of the most magnificent exotic foliage plants for garden or container is *Agave americana*. At Bourton House the yellow-edged cultivar *A. a.* 'Variegata' is planted with *Helichrysum petiolare*

Container-grown displays of foliage plants are more maintenance intensive than a garden border; plants must be watered regularly, fed routinely (with a foliar feed if possible), and groomed daily to remove faded leaves and flowers.

'Limelight' and the succulent *Echeveria harmsii*, which has yellow-lipped crimson flowers. *Agave americana* is coloured blue-grey, and the saw-toothed leaves are fogged with a soft powdery bloom: apart from *A. a.* 'Variegata', there are two other striped cultivars: *A. a.* 'Marginata', with white variegation, and *A. a.* 'Mediopicta', with yellow stripes down the centre of each leaf.

In a grand assemblage at the entrance to the house, a number of pots are gathered together at the foot of a terracotta urn which is planted up with the peppermint-scented geranium used elsewhere and three widely contrasting foliage plants: *Phormium tenax* with its tough strappy leaves; *Salvia confertiflora* with its oval leaves with a felted texture; and *Melianthus major*, barely visible behind the sage, which has segmented leaves coloured a pleasing bloomy blue-grey. This really is a plant worth going out of your way for, unless the scent of the leaves, reminiscent of burnt chocolate, is not to your liking.

Showy displays like this really do make the most of the foliage of tender plants, but to maintain the eye-popping quality the plants must be tended daily. Most of the ones used in these pots prefer well-drained soil and will grow in semi-shade. Remember that some of the plants you use will be rainforest natives, so will want humidity and low light, while others, like agave, salvia and melianthus, don't mind sun and parched conditions. Take the time to familiarize yourself with your plants' requirements. Other counsels of perfection are attention to watering, as some pots will have to be watered twice a day; sluice down the pot as well. Pinch out the growing tips of the plants to keep them in good shape and to encourage bushiness. One of the goals of container gardening with tender foliage plants is to maintain a full and healthy display over a much longer season than you could ever achieve with familiar hardy flowering plants, so feed the plants regularly as watering will leach out the nutrients in composts; foliar feeds are especially good to use in this situation because they are formulated to meet the needs of leafy plants.

A hosta border

In early spring the gardens at Hadspen House in Somerset resume their delicate colour harmonies, and the hosta borders show how to make the best use of this favourite foliage perennial.

Massed plantings of one genus can be quite awe-inspiring and that is certainly the case here, with dozens of different hosta cultivars used to edge a garden path. White-variegated forms mingle with yellow-variegated, and broad-leaved, glaucous-blue varieties contrast with narrow-leaved, acid-green ones. Hostas are at their peak in summer, but unlike many herbaceous perennials they contribute to the garden scene from the moment the foliage begins to unwrap itself until the final meltdown of the last faded leaf. Early in the season, before the plants unfurl their leaves, the space between can be occupied by spring-flowering bulbs; at Hadspen, miniature daffodils and pure yellow tulips are used along with the yellow-variegated grass *Hakonechloa macra* 'Alboaurea', planted in clumps towards the front of the border. The head of the path is framed by *Euphorbia characias, Nectaroscordum siculum* (a bulb in the allium family, with pendant, bell-shaped flowers coloured white and flushed plum down the centre of each petal) and bronze fennel *Foeniculum vulgare* 'Purpureum'. As the season progresses, the faded bulbs vanish beneath the shade of the spreading hosta leaves.

Hostas vary in colour from glaucous blue to acid green and almost yellow, with variegations in assorted distributions – edgings, splashes, midrib streaks – and shades of white, cream and yellow. One of the most popular is glaucous-blue *H.* 'Frances Williams' with pale biscuity beige edges. *H.* 'Blue Umbrellas', *H.* 'Blue Angel' and the heavily textured *H.* 'Love Pat' are among the best blue-greys. The series named for the garden have, in the case of *H.* 'Hadspen Blue', *H.* 'Hadspen Hawk' and *H.* 'Hadspen Heron', glaucous-blue foliage, while *H.* 'Hadspen Samphire' has yellow, lanceolate leaves. *H.* 'Sum and Substance' has huge golden leaves, while *H.* 'Sun Power' is one of the few yellow-leaved hostas that will tolerate a few hours of direct sun each day. *H.* 'Shade Fanfare', *H.* 'Wide Brim' and *H.* 'Nancy Lindsay' all have yellow variegation. *H.* 'Patriot' is one of the brightest white variegated hostas with large, heart-shaped leaves that are emerald green in the centre and edged with broad borders of snowy white; *H.* 'Frosted Jade', *H.* 'Francee' and *H.* 'Big Boy' also have large leaves with white variegation.

On the whole, hostas require a semi-shaded position in well-drained soil which does not dry out. Yellow-leaved and variegated hostas require more shade as the leaves tend to scorch in sun. Cool, moist conditions are particularly important in warmer climates, but in cooler regions hostas will tolerate dry (not arid) conditions helped by their fleshy roots.

The Hadspen gardens are made in an old walled vegetable garden situated on a gentle south-facing slope. To overcome the sun-drenched environment the Popes planted a hornbeam avenue and in autumn the hornbeam leaves fall on to the border, helping to maintain humus levels. In the summertime, when the sun scorches the surrounding borders, a stroll down the shady length of this leafy tunnel provides the garden visitor with welcome and refreshing respite.

The hosta border at Hadspen House in Somerset is only part of the long, double borders (*opposite*) devoted to plants with yellow leaves and flowers. The cultivars suggested in this plan would produce a similar effect: I *Euphorbia characias*; II *Hosta* 'Gold Standard'; III *Hosta* 'Sum and Substance'; IV *Tulipa* 'Yellow Purissima' (Fosteriana hybrid); V *Hosta* 'Aureomarginata'; VI *Hosta* 'Green Gold'; VII *Hosta* 'Royal Standard'; VIII *Hosta* 'Frances Williams'; IX *Hosta* 'Kabitan'; X *Hosta* 'Phyllis Campbell'; XI *Hosta* 'Albo-picta'; XII *Hosta* 'Aureomaculata'; XIII *Hakonechloa* 'Alboaurea' XIV *Hosta sieboldii* 'Alba'.

A bog garden

oliage plants and water features are an especially attractive combination. The still surface of a garden pond will mirror the shapes and textures of overhanging foliage, thereby enhancing the effect of a well-planted bog garden.

A bog garden is one in which the soil is permanently wet, and a boggy area is usually included in the construction of modern artificial garden ponds by lowering one edge of the pond so that water seeps into a specially prepared trench running alongside. The pond liner fabric needs to be large enough to overlap the trench, and while care must be taken not to puncture the actual pond area of the liner, holes are poked through the part of the liner that will be underneath the bog garden compost, which contains plenty of moisture-holding humus or peat. The same effect can be achieved when making a formal pool.

One of the most magnificent of all the marginal plants to grow at the water's edge is *Gunnera manicata*, and in the garden at Hadspen House a single plant sets the stage for a composition which makes the most of contrasts in size. The leaves of a mature gunnera can reach 1.5m (5ft) across, while a plant grown in optimum conditions will easily make 2.5m (8ft) – sheltering beneath one on a rainy day can give you the distinct impression of being in a tropical jungle. The vast lobed leaves have a bristly surface, as does the thick stalk; the flowers form at the heart of the plant and look like giant pine cones. *G. tinctoria* has more rounded leaves with shorter stalks, but will still give substance to a bog-garden planting scheme.

Gunneras like sun as well as deep moist soil, and although they are fairly hardy it is a good idea to give the resting crowns protection in winter; when the leaves fade, fold them inwards to cover the crown, apply a thick blanket of well-rotted manure or compost and cover with bracken if you live in an area in which winters are particularly severe.

Rodgersias also offer some excellent foliage plants and *Rodgersia pinnata* 'Superba' is probably the finest, with segmented, heavily textured leaves that are tinted rich mahogany purple. It grows to about 90cm (3ft) in height from creeping underground rhizomes, and will accept sun or semi-shade, but must have cool moisture at the roots. Similarly, *R. podophylla* has segmented leaves, each leaflet being roughly triangular in shape with serrated edges. Young leaves have a rich chocolatey tint, fading to green for summer and resuming a brownish tinge as they mature.

Darmera peltata, formerly known as *Peltiphyllum peltatum*, has round, crinkly leaves with scalloped edges, about 30cm (12in) across, that are held aloft to about 60cm (2ft) on thick stems. The naked flower stems make a curious sight, rising like a fakir's snakes above the leafy mound. It will gradually colonize a bog garden by creeping rhizomatous roots, but can be controlled by ripping out chunks as necessary. *D. p.* 'Nana', as you might expect, is a smaller version with purple-tinted leaves that are closer to the ground reaching to about 20cm (8in).

With all these broad rounded shapes, it is a good idea to add a counterpoint by the use of a single contrasting shape, as provided here by narrow-leaved plants like *Carex elata* 'Aurea' and *Iris sibirica* 'Snow Queen'. *Miscanthus sinensis* 'Variegatus' is another narrow-leaved plant which provides bright contrast. It is one of the oldest cultivars of miscanthus and carries its white-striped leaves in loose clumps. In autumn the foliage pales to an attractive almond colour. It is surprisingly shade tolerant and in hot climates it is advisable to plant in light shade to prevent leaf burn. One often sees gardener's garters (*Phalaris arundinacea* var. *picta*) used in or near bog gardens; a better common name would be 'gardener's torment' for its invasive nature can be just that. The cultivar *P. a.* var. *picta* 'Feesey' is more brilliantly white, and supposedly less invasive.

Above A planting scheme inspired by Hadspen includes: I *Gunnera manicata*; II *Darmera peltata*; III *Carex elata* 'Aurea'; IV *Hosta sieboldiana*; V *Geranium* 'Johnson's Blue'; VI *Iris sibirica* 'Snow Queen'.
Left The whippy flower stems of *Darmera peltata* echo the linear foliage of *Carex elata* 'Bowles Gold' and siberian iris, and contrast with the rounded shapes of the remaining foliage.

A woodland edge garden

The cool dappled shade to be found at the edge of a woodland provides excellent growing conditions for a wide range of shrubs and perennials that are valuable for their foliage as well as their flower colour.

Anne Waring has exploited this fact in the marvellous leafy patchwork she has created in her West Sussex garden 'North Springs' by mingling a wide range of trees, shrubs and perennial plants in an informal planting. The layered planting of the garden helps it to merge effortlessly into the woodland setting: the verticals of the surrounding trees are brought into the garden by the upright shapes from a range of conifers. Other evergreens provide a permanent anchor for the island perennial beds: *Pieris japonica*, *Mahonia lomariifolia* and *Berberis* cultivars all have strong forms, good foliage shape and interesting textures. Deciduous shrubs to fill out the background planting include variegated *Weigela praecox* 'Variegata' and *Cornus mas*, with bright green leaves, or *C. m.* 'Variegata'. The spindleberry *Euonymus alatus* makes an attractive spreading shrub that takes on fiery autumn colours. Beneath this sheltering layer a path winds between clumps of hosta: by using variegated varieties and cultivars, as Anne has, you can introduce a

Above A planting plan suggested by the woodland edge garden at North Springs includes: I *Angelica archangelica*; II *Polemonium caeruleum*; III *Hosta sieboldiana*; IV *Iris pseudacorus*; V *Lysichiton americanus*; VI *Ligularia dentata* 'Desdemona'; VII *Senecio smithii*; VIII *Symphytum* 'Goldsmith'; IX *Filipendula ulmaria* 'Aurea'; X *Filipendula purpurea*; XI *Hosta crispula*; XII *Trollius* x *cultorum* 'Superbus'; XIII *Hosta undulata* var. *univittata*; XIV *Bergenia* 'Bressingham White'; XV *Hosta* 'Gold Standard'; XVI *Rodgersia pinnata*; XVII *Symphytum* x *uplandicum* 'Variegatum'; XVIII *Lysimachia punctata*.
Opposite The layered approach to planting the woodland garden at North Springs evokes a natural informality while simultaneously providing the right conditions for plants to flourish.

range of tints to which other foliage plants can be related. *Hosta undulata* var. *univittata* has bold white streaks that are repeated in the leaves of *Symphytum* x *uplandicum* 'Variegatum' and *Astrantia major* 'Sunningdale Variegated'; *Hosta* 'Gold Standard' is splashed with yellow, as is *Symphytum* 'Goldsmith', this colour being emphasized by groundcovering plants like *Lysimachia nummularia* 'Aurea' and glowing clumps of *Filipendula ulmaria* 'Aurea'.

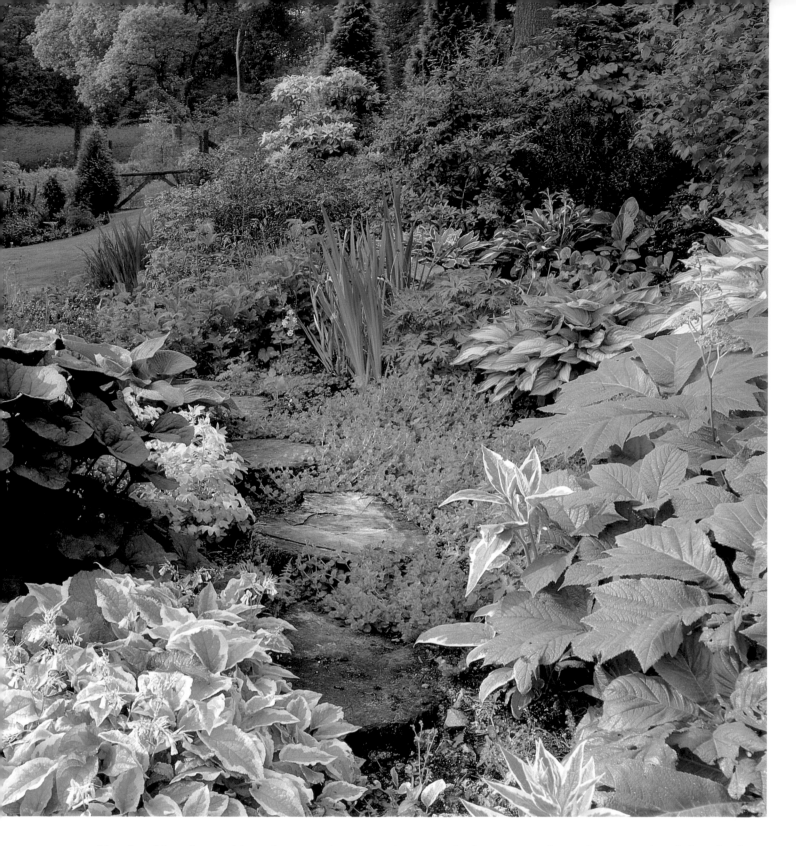

Many broad-leaved perennials need moist conditions to perform well and to keep the foliage in good condition. especially if they in their turn are expected to provide shade for groundcovers. *Rodgersia pinnata* and *Ligularia dentata* 'Desdemona' provide good dense colour in the garden with their vinous purple undersides. but both will droop dismally when the soil begins to dry out. Even more demanding are *Lysichiton americanus* (skunk cabbage).

with glossy tapering leaves that appear long before the flower spathe. and *Senecio smithii*. which has the same high-gloss finish: both prefer to have their roots in water. The reflective surfaces of plants like these bring the brightness of indirect light into a shaded area: *Acanthus mollis* (bear's breeches) is another glossy-leaved perennial with particularly strong architectural foliage. a feature it shares with the herb *Angelica archangelica*.

A dry sunny garden

In complete contrast to the moist conditions found in a woodland garden, this garden enjoys freely draining soil and a sun-baked south-facing aspect. Sandwiched between the hills rising up behind the French village of Giverny and the Loire river, the garden occupies the site of the old vegetable garden. The house, which is next door to Monet's, was once occupied by Leila Cabot Perry, who was a patroness of the American Impressionists. The house and garden are undergoing restoration, with the garden project under the direction of the garden designer Mark Brown.

When restoring the flower garden area in front of the house, Mark studied the paintings of Frederick Carl Frieseke which show the garden as it was when Mrs Cabot Perry was in residence. There are rose borders and many colourful annuals; the lawn is studded with dwarf apple trees and edged by a perennial border and step-over

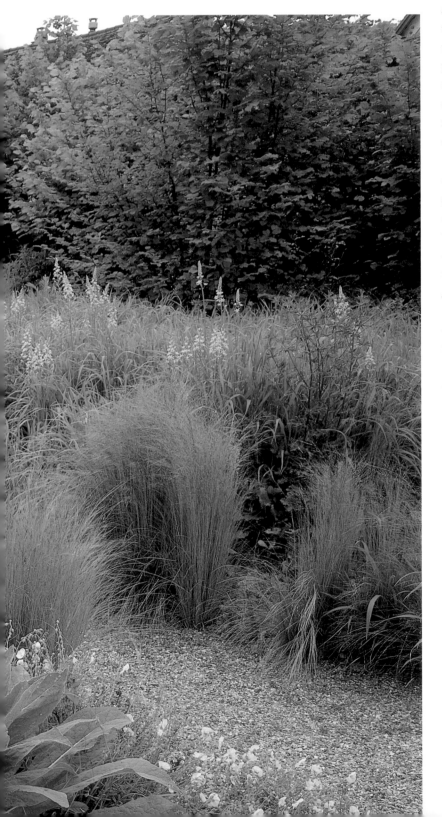

apple hedge. Adjacent to this formal part of the garden there was a derelict kitchen garden which received a very different treatment. Its entirely new design and planting reflects Mark's abiding interest in naturally occurring plant *biomes*, the term used in France to express the idea of grouping plants according to their ability to accept the same conditions of soil and light. Taking his lead from the flora of the hills above the village, Mark has created a garden of grasses and herbs suited to a sun-filled site. The ground is warm and well-drained and ideal for the sages, verbascums, catmints, marjorams, thymes and other perennial herbs that are woven into the grassy matrix of blue-green *Sesleria caerulea* in the centre of the garden and *Brachypodium distachyon* in the perimeter areas.

There are gardeners who disregard the potential of grasses, seeing them only as a voguish plant which will eventually be surpassed by another as garden fashion changes. However, with ecology and conservation high on the agenda, the horticultural world is increasingly concerned with establishing energy-efficient gardens which are compatible with existing conditions. It must be acknowledged that there are few plants as adaptable to a variety of moods and settings as grass, and also few that will provide such a varied and pleasing display over such a long season. From early spring when fresh green shoots begin to emerge through summer flowering and seed-forming to late autumn when burnished reds and browns replace the verdant green, ornamental grasses mark the changes of season like no other herbaceous plant.

Apart from the seslaria and brachypodium which are the foundation planting of the garden, there are a number of other showy grasses given prominence, including clumps of feather-fine *Stipa tenuissima* and its splendid relation *S. gigantea*. Stipas are among the most graceful grasses in the garden: early in the season *S. tenuissima* holds itself erect, but as the fine silky seedheads begin to form it droops to make a filmy mound of warm golden tints. *S. gigantea*, however, sends up erect flowers stems to about 60cm (2ft) from which dangle the large oat-shaped seedheads that glitter and bob in the lightest breeze. Both plants are easy to propagate from seed: with *S. tenuissima* you simply comb out the filamented seedheads and spread the mass evenly on the surface of a trayful of compost. Sieve a thin layer of compost over the top, water gently and leave to germinate in semi-shaded spot. Prick out in small clumps into separate pots or line out in nursery beds. *S. gigantea* seeds can be handled individually by the long corkscrew-twisted filament and sown in trays. Another graceful oat-type grass in the garden is *Chasmanthium latifolium*, a native of North America much loved for its graceful dangling panicles of broad flat seeds that stir in the slightest breeze.

Bamboos feature in the garden also, used to shade a seating area at one end of a wisteria-covered pergola and at the furthest end of the garden to make a shelter belt which serves as a noise baffle, cutting the intrusive decibels generated by the busy main road beyond the garden walls. Apart from its graceful habit, bamboo has music and movement – from the sound and sway of its leaves and canes stirring in the breeze – and mystery: a bamboo grove creates a

Mark Brown drew inspiration from the south-facing slopes of the hills behind Giverny to create this tranquil oasis of herbs and grasses. In late summer when the herbs bloom, the garden drifts in a soft blue sea of flower colour enhanced by the blue-grey foliage that predominates.

shadowy mass through which bright sun can only trickle. The canes of some cultivars and species of the genus *Phyllostachys* have the most subtle colourings, from the dark, cocoa-brown of mature *P. nigra* to the sunny yellow of *P. aurea* 'Holochrysa'. There are variegated stem colourings also: *P. vivax* 'Aureocaulis' has green and yellow markings, while *P. nigra* 'Boryana' is blotched with brown. *P. flexuosa* is the Chinese weeping bamboo, with dark purple canes: it needs plenty of space.

As autumn arrives the grasses become a warm tint of honey gold enamelled with the cobalt-blue flowers of *Catananche caerula*, *Nepeta* 'Six Hills Giant', *Perovskia atriplicifolia* and numerous other hillside herbs, which then leave behind the burnished umbels, panicles and pods that are full of next year's promise.

Left The angel-hair delicacy of *Stipa tenuissima* is in pointed contrast to the agressive shape of the wild thistle growing in its midst.
Opposite The texture of the erect stems of hyssop, lychnis, perovskia and *Stipa gigantea* blend together, but the plants form distinct layers of colour.
Below Dry gardens and gravel paths lend themselves to this kind of natural habitat-influenced gardening. Plants used are: I *Paeonia lactiflora* 'White Wings'; II *Nepeta* x *faassenii*; III *Catananche caerulea* 'Major'; IV *Sesleria caerula*; V *Stipa gigantea*; VI *Salvia pratensis*; VII *Helianthemum* 'The Bride'; VIII *Verbascum nigrum*; IX *Stipa tenuissima*; X *Cynoglossum nervosum*; XI *Echinops ritro*; XII *Brachypodium distachyon*; XIII *Asphodelus albus*.

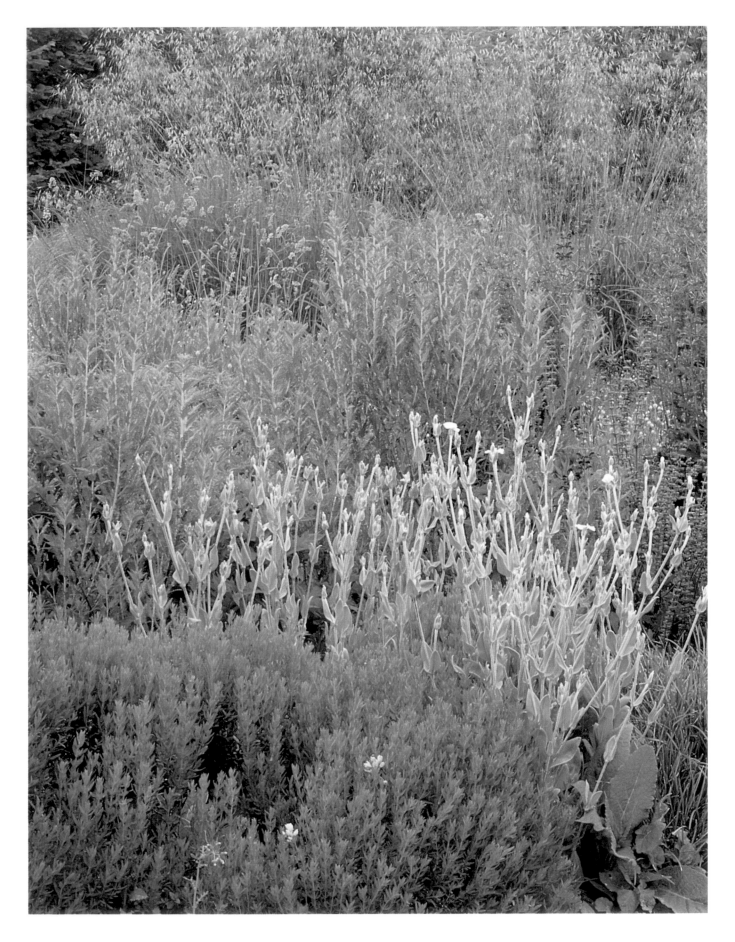

A late season shrub garden

A friend of mine who lives in Boston sent me a photograph of her winter garden. All one could make out were lumpen white shapes like toppled snowmen, hinting that there was indeed something under all that snow. It might have been a shrub, or it could have been a dustbin. When conditions are that extreme, there is little to do but long for the thaw, but Sally's reminder of what gardening can be like did make me appreciate anew how the colour of bark on various trees and shrubs can brighten a garden in even the most remorseless winter.

There are certain shrubs that leap instantly to mind which are dependably hardy (even under a frosty shroud) and top of the list are the coloured-stem dogwoods. *Cornus alba* 'Argenteo-Marginata' has bright crimson stems and the added summer feature of variegated foliage; *C. a.* 'Sibirica' has ruby-red stems; and *C. a.* 'Kesselringii' has purplish-black stems. *C. a.* 'Spaethii' and *C. a.* 'Westonbirt' can also be relied upon to colour well in leaf and stem, as can *C. a.* 'Aurea', which has buttery-yellow autumn foliage on dark red stems. One other species worth noting is *C. stolonifera* 'Flaviramea' which has egg-yolk yellow stems.

Other popular shrubs are the scarlet willow (*Salix daphnoides*) and the yellow willow (*S. alba vitallina*). Even the weeping willow (*S.* 'Chrysocoma') has the most delicate yellow tint on its new growth. The violet willow (*Salix alba vitellina* 'Britzensis') has a soft silvery bloom that turns the purple bark nearly white. Another shrub with a curious sheen on its stems is *Elaeagnus commutata*, which looks as though it has been dusted over with gold. Combined with the leathery silver-grey leaves it makes quite a show, as does its relative *E. angustifolia*, which has delightful coppery fruit in dense clusters along the stems and long tapering grey leaves.

There are a few other good bright whites for shrub stem colour and among the best are two silver-stemmed brambles. *Rubus cockburnianus* and *R. thibetanus*: the first is a much stronger white, but the latter's cultivar *R. t.* 'Silver Fern' has particularly pretty foliage perfectly described by the name. The Japanese wineberry (*R. phoenicolasius*) has crimson stems densely covered in prickly little thorns; the undersides of the leaves are nicely silvered, so the plant is attractive for much of the year.

Using this collection of shrubs as a point of departure, and drawing inspiration from the gardens scenes shown here, I can imagine planting a winter corner that would be set alight by the low slanting sun of that season.

Most of the shrubs grow to about 1.2m (5ft) so I would include a tree or two for height, probably the spectral white birch *Betula jacquemontii* 'Jermyns'. The best effect is had by growing it as a multi-stemmed specimen. However, if that would be too startling, the soft red bark of *Acer pensylvanicum* 'Erythrocladum' could provide a warming glow. *Acer griseum* is the paperbark maple, and its peeling bark has an equally warm cinnamon tint.

Opposite: Massed plantings of dogwood cultivars make a vibrant and demanding frame filled with perennials chosen for their leaf textures and harmonizing colour. The plants suggested in the plan *(above)* are: I *Cornus alba* 'Westonbirt'; II *Cornus florida* 'Rainbow'; III *Bergenia crassifolia*; IV *Rubus biflorus*; V *Cornus alba* 'Spaethii'; VI *Hebe pinguifolia* 'Pagei'; VII *Ajuga reptans* 'Purpurea'; VIII *Rubus phoenicolasus*; IX *Hamamelis* x *intermedia* 'Jelena'; X *Cornus alba* 'Aurea'; XI *Symphytum* x *uplandicum* 'Variegatum'; XII *Chamaecyparis lawsoniana* 'Winston Churchill'; XIII *Cornus stolonifera* 'Flaviramea'; XIV *Parthenocissus tricuspidata*.

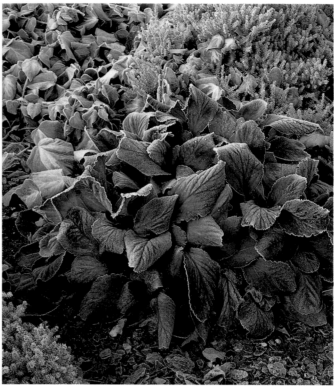

Left Acer rubrum foliage brings a bold splash of colour to autumn plantings. *Right* There are many groundcovers, like *Bergenia crassifolia*, that colour well. *Opposite* Evergreens add depth to a predominantly deciduous group of trees.

There are any number of winter-colouring groundcovers to lay beneath the shrubs and one of the darkest is *Ajuga reptans* 'Atropurpurea', which remains solidly purple through every kind of weather. *Parthenocissus tricuspidata* becomes a glossy flame-red mantle to spread on the ground or to throw over a wall. Other groundcovers could include *Nandina domestica* 'Wood's Dwarf', a semi-evergreen (or rather ever-brown) dwarf shrub commonly called the sacred bamboo which would appreciate the shelter of the taller-growing shrubs.

Using an evergreen or two would give depth to the planting: perhaps *Chamaecyparis lawsoniana* 'Winston Churchill', as shown here, or, if less of an exclamation mark is needed - merely a full stop - the tidy little *Cryptomeria japonica* 'Globosa Nana'. Bright shrubs with a touch of gold would bring the image of dappled light and shade and so give depth to the collection of stem and branch: either one of the hollies, perhaps *Ilex aquifolium* 'Bacciflava', with its yellow berries, another elaeagnus, *Elaeagnus pungens* 'Maculata', or, as groundcover, *Euonymus fortunei* 'Emerald 'n' Gold'.

Including a winter-flowering shrub, particularly in a walled garden where the scent would be less likely to blow away on the breeze, would add another layer of interest. For my money I would include a witch hazel, such as *Hamamelis* x *intermedia* 'Jelena' shown here. It is an orange-flowered cultivar of the familiar yellow-flowered species, with which it shares the same ethereal perfume. Witch hazel has pleasing autumn leaf colours, and a member of the same *Hamamelidaceae* family, *Disanthus cercidifolius*, has foliage that colours crimson and wine-red in autumn.

Colourfully stemmed plants need help to remain so, and the way to do this is to prune away the old growth to encourage new stems, since it is the new growth that has the best colour. The ideal time to do this is in the early spring, just as the sap begins to rise. That way you will have enjoyed the colourful stems all autumn and winter, and will be setting the stage for the next season's display.

Some people recommend 'stooling' which means removing absolutely every stick to leave behind a cluster of five or so stumps from which new growth will shoot. If the shrubs play an important structural role in the garden you may not want to remove so much, so the best thing to do is to remove only about one-third of the branches, beginning with the oldest wood. This is easy to recognize as it will have the darkest colour and be the thickest branches in the shrub. (You may have to use a good pruning saw or parrot-nose loppers rather than secateurs.) Then remove any other growth that is damaged or tangled to leave a neat, open shape.

Right Be bold with foliage plants in a small garden; you will find the dramatic effects and air of repose they create is a far more satisfying – and long-lasting – display than a collection of plants chosen for their comparatively short-lived flower colour alone.

Below A narrow path beneath a canopy of evergreen and brightly coloured foliage is edged with a variety of shade-loving shrubs, gold-variegated grasses like *Cortaderia selloana* 'Sunstripe' and *Hakonechloa macra* 'Alboaurea' and ground-covering ivies and tolmeia.

A courtyard garden

Sonny Garcia's small garden in northern California makes the most of its space by an abundant use of foliage. There are more than 150 different plants ranging from Chusan palms (*Trachycarpus fortunei*) to ground-covering *Tolmiea menziesii* 'Taff's Gold', but even with this widely varying display, the leafy theme ensures that there is a feeling of quiet repose. The layers of planting, with their individual themes of contrast in leaf form and colour, create their own rhythms. Drifts of grasses like the variegated *Cortaderia selloana* 'Sunstripe' and *Hakonechloa macra* 'Alboaurea' skirt the edges of the paved paths, softening the hard edges with rounded shapes created by the mass of arching leaves.

Grasses add a sort of music to the garden, rustling like silken skirts disturbed by a passing breeze. This gentle sound enhances even further the tranquillity of the garden and makes a satisfying substitute for water, a favourite 'musical' accessory in garden design. Bamboo has a similar sound effect and could be used to create an effective screen, or to create a shady shelter belt beneath which contrasting low spreading shapes could be effectively brought into play. *Phyllostachys nigra* grows to only 3.5m (12ft), with bright green young stems aging to black: using this to create strong verticals and contrasting its narrow ribbon leaves with the feathery fronds of *Aruncus dioicus* with a groundcover of a broad-leaved plant like hosta, perhaps the variegated *H. undulata* var. *univittata* would make a soothing garden corner.

In this garden, most of the larger shrubs have the most striking foliage as though to emphasize their importance as screens and backdrops to the groupings of lower-growing shrubs and herba-

Below A planting plan that incorporates many of Sonny Garcia's design principles. I *Prunus cerasifera pissardii*; II *Cyathea cooperi*; III *Hakenechloa macra*; IV *Cordyline australis* 'Albertii'; V *Acer pseudoplatanus* 'Prinz Handjery'; VI *Cortaderia selloana* 'Sunstripe'; VII Rhododendron; VIII Magnolia; IX Chusan palm (*Trachycarpus fortunei*); X *Lonicera nitida* 'Baggesen's Gold'; XI *Spiraea japonica* 'Goldflame'; XII *Cotinus coggygria*; XIII Apple espalier.

ceous plants with more subtle characters. There are rhododendrons with variegated leaves (always a good choice, since most plants within this group leave a boring dull green gap in a planting once their springtime flower show is over). There is also a *Magnolia* x *soulangeana*; unlike the evergreen rhododendrons, it sheds its leaves, which reappear after the spring flush of pink-tinted flowers. Their broad heavy nature combine well to make a shady enclave.

The shrubs seem to carry the colour message with tints of bronze-purple and yellow being the main theme. *Acer palmatum* 'Atropurpureum', *Prunus cerasifera* 'Pissardii', *Cotinus coggygria* 'Royal Purple' and *Phormium* 'Dark Delight' are the most predominantly dark tinted foliage plants. There are a number of yellow variegated plants scattered throughout, with *Cortaderia selloana* 'Sunstripe' and *Cordyline australis* 'Albertii' bursting like sunspots through the clouds of foliage. *Lonicera nitida* 'Baggesen's Gold' and

Spiraea japonica 'Goldflame' are common yellow-leaved shrubs; more unusual is *Acer psuedoplatanus* 'Prinz Handjery', which has shrimp pink juvenile leaves that change to green as they age. With such a dense planting, the groundcover shrubs must be shade tolerant like the yellow variegated ivy *Hedera helix* 'Golden Child', which also brings brightness to shady depths, and *Liatris spicata*.

In a garden of this size (roughly 10 x 15m/35 x 50ft) it is necessary to prune hard – but thoughtfully – on a regular basis, not just to keep the garden from being overwhelmed, but also to keep the plants in good health. Close planting encourages etiolated growth, when new leaves and stems appear thin and drawn, and such growth is susceptible to disease. So pruning to control size will improve the condition of the new growth, which will be healthy and well-formed. This is particularly relevant to plants grown specifically for their foliage as new branches always carry the best leaves.

PROPAGATION

THE PRACTICAL SIDE OF GARDENING IS NEVER FAR AWAY from the aesthetic concerns of planning and planting. In the case of a garden that makes the utmost use of foliage and stem colour in massed plantings, propagation will be a prime concern; if carpets of foliage are not the main objective you may still want to increase stocks of a choice plant in your collection, or renew plantings that are beginning to deteriorate with age. It is also satisfying to share your plants with fellow gardeners, and if you open your garden to visitors plant sales can bring in extra revenue allowing you scope to increase your range of plants with new purchases.

Plants fall into several categories and within those categories various methods of propagation suit certain plants better than others. Working on the principle that it is always best to understand the whys as well as the wherefores, I have included here a potted primer of seed, stem and leaf physiology; I believe an understanding of theory always helps practice to succeed.

In late summer, the flower spikes of the marginal water plant, *Pontaderia cordata*, are protected by their cloaks of bright glossy foliage. It is one of the few blue-flowered aquatics and may be propagated by division in spring.

Annuals

There are two sorts of annual plants, hardy annuals and half-hardy annuals. Both complete their life cycle in one year but the former are grown from seed sown *in situ* in spring or early autumn and the latter are sown under glass in late winter or early spring, usually with heat to aid germination, and then planted out when all danger of frost is past.

Biennials

These grow and produce leaves in the first season then flower and die in the next. Seed is usually sown in summer in prepared seedbeds, then the plants are put out in their flowering positions the following spring. They can also be reproduced vegetatively, by cuttings.

Perennials

These plants live for many years. They include herbaceous perennials (including bulbs, corms and tubers) which have a permanent root system but soft top growth that dies back annually; evergreen woody perennials, which have a permanent root system supporting a permanent woody structure that retains the leaves in winter; and deciduous woody perennials, which have the permanent root system and woody structure, but lose their leaves in winter. Perennials are usually reproduced vegetatively, although growing from seed is possible.

Seeds

Reproducing plants from the seed contained within berries and other capsules is a plant's method of sexual reproduction; all other methods like cuttings and divisions are vegetative. If you want to be sure of obtaining new plants which are identical to the old, you should use one of the vegetative methods described. Pollination is random if left to birds and insects, but by mixing the pollen of different species or making a selection within a species of individuals possessed of particularly fine qualities you can create new hybrids or cultivars respectively.

Flower structure

Seed from all sorts of plants can be sown and germinated with varying degrees of success, but to have seed you must have flowers. In order to understand the process of seed development and germination, it helps to know a little about flower structure.

Most flowers are hermaphrodites, containing male and female reproductive parts; some plants have separate male and female flowers on the same plant, while other plants are strictly single sex, either male or female. To obtain seed from the latter, you must have one plant of each sex.

The main parts of a flower are the petals, which are usually brightly coloured and have scent glands to attract insects to aid pollination. They are arranged in a corolla, or ring, and each petal will have lines or grooves called honey guides which will lead the insect into the flower.

At the base of the flower are the sepals, forming the calyx, which protects the juvenile flower in bud. Inside the flower are the stamens, made up of the pollen-bearing anthers supported on filaments which hold the anthers in the best position to transfer pollen (the male reproductive cell) to insects or to be caught by a breeze; when the pollen is ripe, the anthers split open to release it. Stamens are the male reproductive organs and are held in the part of the flower called the androecium.

The female parts are located in the very heart of the flower. The stigma receives the ripe pollen and so is often sticky and feathery to aid the transfer; the style is a tube through which the pollen travels from the stigma to the ovary, which contains one or more ovules (the female reproductive cells). At the base of the ovaries are nectaries which produce nectar to attract insects and birds. The seeds are formed in the receptacle, at the point where the stalk and flower meet.

Pollination

There are two kinds of pollination: cross-pollination, when the pollen from one plant pollinates another, and self-pollination, when a plant pollinates its own flowers. There are two methods of cross-pollination – insect (which includes birds, slugs, snails or other living creatures that effect the transfer of pollen) and wind pollination. Plants which rely on insect pollination have large, brightly coloured or scented flowers, or a combination of these features. The anthers are small, on short filaments, and produce small quantities of pollen. The individual pollen grains have spiky surfaces so that they attach easily to passing insects. The stigma is also small and held deep within the plant. Wind pollinators generally have small, inconspicuous flowers without scent or nectar, and the anthers are held aloft on long filaments where they dangle like tiny lanterns. They make a bigger quantity of large, light pollen grains which are easily caught by the large feathery anthers that protrude outside the body of the flower.

Fertilization

Fertilization is the fusion of the pollen grain (male gamete) and the ovule (female gamete) when the pollen grain lands on the stigma (*Fig. 5*). Each gamete contains half the genetic information. Chemicals on the stigma will recognize whether or not the pollen is acceptable, so preventing unsuitable cross-pollination between plant types. The pattern of the pollen must also match the pattern on the stigma to ensure the two will marry. Finally, there must be moisture.

If these conditions are met, the pollen produces a tube which grows down the style, absorbing nutrients as it goes, until it reaches the ovary where it penetrates an ovule at the micropyle, a small hole in the ovule. When that process is successfully completed, a pollen grain is released and moves down the tube into the ovule. There the male and female gametes fuse to form a zygote, an entire cell which starts to divide and ultimately become a seed (*Fig. 5*).

As soon as the flower is successfully fertilized it falls away or shrivels up, sometimes leaving the sepals behind. The developing zygote emits a hormone that induces the ovary to swell and become a fruit – either a fleshy berry or a dry, hard capsule. Brightly coloured berries attract birds which then carry the seed in their gut, 'sowing' it in their droppings around the garden; small animals take berries, nuts and other dry seeds, and either bury them in caches or otherwise scatter the seed about the garden; and much dry seed is scattered by the wind.

Germination

If the conditions are right and the seed has been sown properly, germination takes place. The seed will begin to absorb moisture from the sowing medium through the micropyle and will grow either quickly if it is warm or slowly if cold (*Fig. 6*). It begins to absorb oxygen and this respiration breaks down the food reserves in the cotyledons, which also serve as the engines of photosynthesis before the first true leaves appear. The root bud, or radicle, elongates and breaks through the testa (the hard coat that protects the seed from diseases) at the micropyle. As the radicle grows it begins to produce lateral roots and root hairs that anchor the seedling and absorb nutrients. As it pushes

through the soil, the very tip of the radicle is protected by a tough little cap.

The hypocotyl, or vestigial stem, then begins to lengthen, which has the effect of pulling the cotyledons out of the soil (*Fig. 6a*). Up to this point the cotyledons have been protecting the plumule of first true leaves from damage but as the plumule increases in size the cotyledons split apart, allowing the leaves to expand on the developing shoot as the hypocotyl continues to lengthen and straighten up from its swan-necked posture (*Fig. 7*). This is the process of germination for dicotyledons (dicots), or plants that have two cotyledons.

Monocotyledons (monocots) – plants with one cotyledon – germinate rather differently (*Fig. 8*). The radicle and the plumule are contained within a sheath called the coleorhiza. The radicle breaks through this and the testa first, then the plumule emerges, wrapped in its coleophile sheath. This sheath splits and the first true leaves emerge.

Most plants are dicots, and in these the cotyledons protrude above the soil to begin photosynthesis. The leaves have a midrib and secondary veins arranged in branched networks. The stem is formed from tidy concentric rings of vascular tissue composed of phloem, xylem and cambium (*Fig. 9*), and there is usually only one true root system, although secondary or adventitious roots are formed by some plants along the stems above ground, allowing the plant to root where it touches the soil and so take in extra nutrients to support more growth. The flowers consist of petals and sepals produced in fours and fives.

Monocot plants have a single cotyledon that is usually left beneath the soil. The leaves are simple single shapes, usually long and tapering, and with parallel veins running the length of the leaf. The vascular bundles are scattered throughout the stem, which is often quite spongy. Roots are fibrous, most often adven-

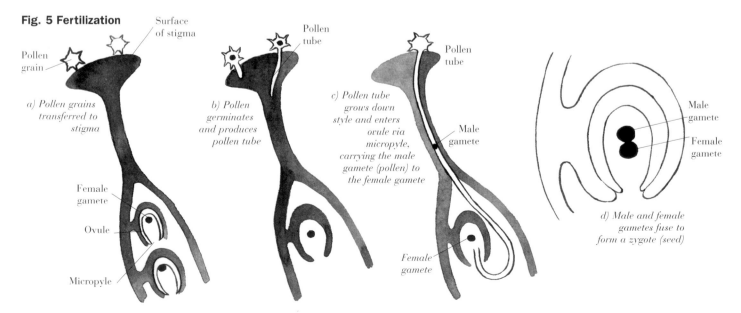

Fig. 5 Fertilization

Surface of stigma

Pollen grain

a) Pollen grains transferred to stigma

Female gamete

Ovule

Micropyle

Pollen tube

b) Pollen germinates and produces pollen tube

Pollen tube

c) Pollen tube grows down style and enters ovule via micropyle, carrying the male gamete (pollen) to the female gamete

Male gamete

Female gamete

Male gamete

Female gamete

d) Male and female gametes fuse to form a zygote (seed)

Fig. 6 Germination

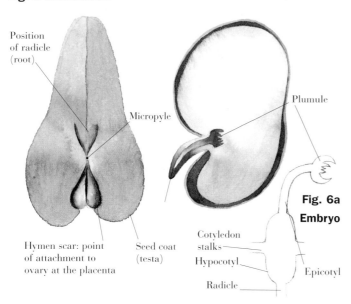

Position of radicle (root)

Micropyle

Plumule

Fig. 6a Embryo

Hymen scar: point of attachment to ovary at the placenta

Seed coat (testa)

Cotyledon stalks

Hypocotyl

Epicotyl

Radicle

titious, and the flower petals and sepals are arranged in threes or groups of three.

Seed may be either dry or moist. Dry seed must be stored in dry conditions and most dry seeds appear to benefit from a period of chilling. Do not store dry seed in plastic bags or containers: use paper envelopes and cardboard boxes kept cool.

Moist seeds (for example oak and chestnut) contain fats as well as the water content and must not be allowed to dry out, as this would either kill the seed or reinforce its dormancy. Moist seed should be put in a mix of equal parts moist sand and peat or between layers of damp sacking and stored in an open airy environment to avoid disease.

Some seeds are trapped within a pulp and can be tricky to extract. The easiest ways to do this are either through maceration – soaking the berries in water to make a quite liquid mash from which the seeds will float to the surface – or else by fermentation, leaving the seed in a sealed plastic bag so that the natural bacteria can break the pulp down.

When a seed does not germinate it may be that it is dormant. Dormancy can be broken in various ways: some plants require high temperatures, and exposure to fire will shatter their sleep; others need a spell of freezing or cold weather and can be stratified (mixed in moist sand and stored outside over winter or else in a refrigerator for a few weeks) to aid germination. Yet others simply need to have their hard coats broken by nicking with a sharp knife, or softened by soaking in hot water to enable the radicle, hypocotyl and cotyledons to emerge.

Sowing seed

The sowing of seed is the most fundamental method of raising new plants, used mostly to raise hardy and half-hardy annuals

and biennials for the garden, though most species of plants can be raised from seeds. Bear in mind that if the plant you are wanting to increase is a hybrid cultivar, seed saved from it will not come true and it will not look like its parent. Instead, it will exhibit some of the characteristics of its parents' parents, perhaps different colouring. In fact, even seed saved from species which will come true may have enhanced leaf colour or variegation, or its natural habit of growth exaggerated, and so on. This is interesting to watch for, since by careful selection you may be able to develop an especially good form of a choice plant.

The best way to sow seed is to fill a pot or tray that has been cleaned thoroughly and washed with a household disinfectant with clean, moist seed compost. Gently firm the compost into the container and then water well. Scatter the seed thinly and evenly over the surface of the compost and then sieve a fine layer of compost over the seed. Water gently (having added fungicide to the water to help prevent the emerging seedling from damping off) and put the pot into a plastic bag or cover the tray with a sheet of glass and put in warm, but not hot, place. Light levels should be low and you can cover the trays with sheets of newspaper to ensure this. There are tabletop propagating units available that have heating cables in the base. These are very useful if you have a place to leave them plugged in.

The seed should germinate in a week to ten days. As soon as you see the seed is germinating and beginning to push through the soil, move the container into the light. If the emerging seeds do not have enough light, they will become etiolated (weak and spindly) and easily damped off.

When the first true leaves (as opposed to the cotyledons) develop, the seedlings are large enough to handle: lift them gently from the compost using the end of a pencil or small seedling dibber. Always hold a seedling by its leaves, never by the stem. A damaged leaf will be replaced by another, but a wounded stem condemns the plant to death.

Fig. 7 Dicotyledon Germination

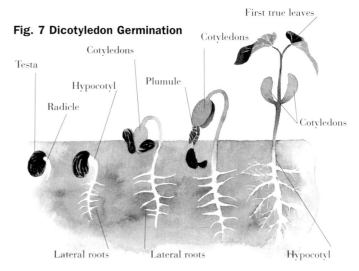

First true leaves

Cotyledons

Cotyledons

Testa

Cotyledons

Hypocotyl

Plumule

Radicle

Cotyledons

Lateral roots

Lateral roots

Hypocotyl

Prick out the individual seedlings of large plants into individual pots; small annuals and so on can be pricked out into rows in trays. Don't overcrowd the trays; to grow into strong plants, the seedlings should be planted no less than about 2.5cm (1in) apart. Overcrowding means the plants must compete for food and light. In a standard seed tray, about five plants across and six down (30 plants) is a good average.

Keep the pricked-out seedlings in the greenhouse for a few days and then, as the weather warms, harden them off by moving the trays and pots outside for a few hours each day, increasing the time they spend in the fresh air as the days become warmer. This is an essential part of the process of raising plants from seed.

Herbaceous perennials grown from seed can flower well in their second season, but there are some which will take several years to reach flowering size. Cultivars and F1 hybrids are unlikely to come true from self-saved seed but species perennials should, although as mentioned earlier there may be variation in the depth of colour or leaf size. Sow the seed in spring or summer on a spare piece of ground, or else in pots set out in a cold frame. With tray-sown seed, thin the seedlings as necessary to allow for strong growth, and when the plants are large enough pot them up into 8cm (3in) pots.

Take a look at the seed; if it is flat it will germinate more readily if you take the time to sow it on its side or edge. Some seeds have long 'tails': if you poke the seed into the compost with this tail protruding, it will spiral as it dries and in the process twist the seed firmly and deeply into the compost.

The Stem

Propagation from stem cuttings is the second most common method after seed; leaf cuttings are less frequently used and tend to be a means of increasing houseplants and exotic ornamentals.

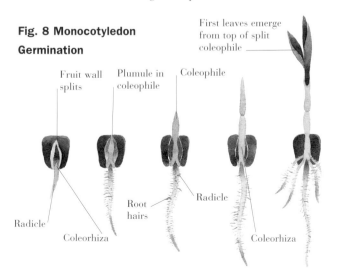

Fig. 8 Monocotyledon Germination

First leaves emerge from top of split coleophile

Fruit wall splits

Plumule in coleophile

Coleophile

Radicle

Root hairs

Radicle

Coleorhiza

Coleorhiza

Being vegetative methods, leaf and stem cuttings are the most widely used way of producing new plants which are guaranteed to be exact replicas of the parent. In addition, where perennial plants are concerned, cuttings produce usable plants more rapidly.

Apart from providing plants with their characteristic forms and shapes, stems serve a number of basic functions. They support the leaves, flowers and buds for optimum light absorption, and to enhance the opportunities for pollination and seed dispersal; leaves are spaced along the stems to receive the best light and most oxygen possible. They are the conduit for water and nutrients from the roots to the leaves and allow for the manufacture and storage of food for all the plant tissue; although most food production (photosynthesis) takes place in the leaves, some takes place in green stems.

On a green stem (*Fig. 8*), the epidermis is a layer of closely fitting cells that holds the inner tissues in shape, prevents water loss and protects the internal structures of the stem against disease and pest damage. The epidermis is punctured with microscopic lenticels through which the plant respires, exchanging oxygen for carbon dioxide. On older woody plant stems, the epidermis gives way to an outer sheath of cork that is several cell layers thick; this is the bark that makes some trees and shrubs highly decorative.

The cortex and the pith consist of large, thin-walled cells separated by air spaces to allow air to move around the tissues of the plant. The cells themselves are water receptacles, and when full help to keep the stem erect (turgid); a plant wilts as these cells empty. The cells also form protective packing around the vascular bundles of phloem and xylem; the phloem allows for the movement of photosynthesized nutrients around the plant, while water and nutrients absorbed by the roots travel to the leaves via the xylem.

The cambium is a layer of thin-walled narrow cells that divides the vascular bundles in half, separating the inner xylem layer from the outer phloem layer. Xylem and phloem are created by the cambium layer, and each year the new layer pushes the old one out, creating the characteristic tree rings seen when a branch is cross-sectioned. Cambium cells have the ability to divide and to produce adventitious roots, so it is from this layer that a cutting develops roots.

The tip of the stem is the apical bud (*Fig. 9a*), containing hormonal active meristem tissue. The point along a stem where the leaves are attached is called the node; meristem stem tissue is also present in the bud at the nodes, nestled between the leaf and the stem. The distance between nodes along a stem is the internode; some plants can be propagated by internodal cuttings (*Fig. 10d*).

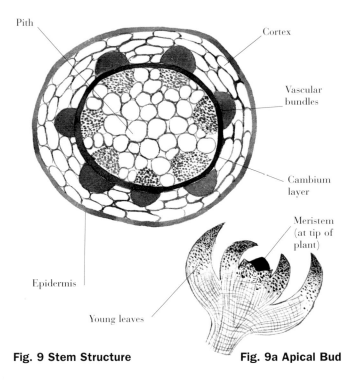

Pith

Cortex

Vascular
bundles

Cambium
layer

Meristem
(at tip of
plant)

Epidermis

Young leaves

Fig. 9 Stem Structure   **Fig. 9a Apical Bud**

Softwood cuttings

These are made from young green shoots. They are particularly good for propagating herbaceous perennials, and can be taken at any time in the season when there is vigorous new growth. Softwood cuttings of trees and shrubs are from the new season's growth taken during spring. Cutting material should be healthy, non-flowering shoots (a plant in flower has its hormones geared to vegetative growth and so is unlikely to produce roots). Take cuttings about 10cm (4in) long, cutting them away from the parent plant just above a node. Collect the cuttings in the early morning while they are turgid; to keep the cuttings in good condition as you gather them, put them in a plastic bag into which you have sprinkled a few drops of water. It is essential to keep the cuttings moist.

Prepare pots and trays as for seed sowing, using your usual compost mix, but add some extra grit or horticultural vermiculite to give it quite an open texture. I do this even if the compost says it is for cuttings, adding horticultural vermiculite in a ratio of one potful of grit to two of compost. Newly developing roots prefer the reduced resistance of an open compost; damp, compacted compost would make the cutting rot off. Do not firm the compost too vigorously as air as well as moisture must be present around the cutting.

To prepare the cutting, trim away the stem below the lowest node as cleanly as you can (*Fig. 10a*), being careful not to squash the end of the stem: I make the cut against my thumb, using a sharp scalpel and a great deal of care. A sharp knife will suffice, but do not use secateurs or scissors. Next, trim away the lowest leaves and any flowers and buds, being careful not to

nick the stem. Cuttings taken during summer should have all but the uppermost two pairs of leaves removed; the reason for this is that during warm weather, leaves lose moisture. Cuttings taken late in the season and during winter or early spring should have a greater number of leaves to absorb all the light possible to continue photosynthesis. If the cutting is taken from a large-leaved plant, cut each leaf in half and dip the cut edge in disinfectant solution to prevent the disease botrytis.

When the cambium is cut it forms a callus which contains cells that differentiate between stem and root. Hormones gather at the cut, activating the root-forming cells. Dipping the cut end into hormone rooting powder or solution assists this process. Tap off any excess rooting agent; too much would kill the cutting.

Use a pencil or small dibber to put the cutting into the compost to about one-third of its depth; the cutting should be deep enough to be secure, with the growth point held cleanly above the compost. Firm the compost around the cuttings and water them in with a fungicide solution.

The cuttings must be kept moist, and if you are planning to produce prodigious numbers of plants you should invest in a mist-propagating unit. These have sensors which periodically engage misting sprays above the bench to ensure a constant moist atmosphere around the cuttings. The bottom of the unit will have a soil-warming cable under the layer of felt or sand on which the pots and trays stand to provide bottom heat which encourages rooting. Otherwise, cover the pots or trays with a

Fig. 10 Stem Cuttings

a) Softwood   *b) Semi-ripe*

Remove
lowest
pairs of
leaves

Node

Cut below
lowest node

Remove
lowest
leaves

Heel

Bark 'tongue'
trim away

Cut at angle
above a bud

Sand in
bottom of
v-shaped
trench

Cut
straight
across
below
bud

Cut to
leave
2.5cm
stem
above
node

Node

Cut below
leaf node

c) Hardwood   *d) Internodal*

polythene bag or half a clear plastic bottle (I find the latter especially good for pots of cuttings). Both methods make a mini greenhouse and keep a moist atmosphere around the cuttings. If it is summer. the ambient heat may be enough but using a propagating unit with bottom heat will speed up the process.

Don't stand cuttings on the sunniest benches: put them where they will be cool and shaded. After a few weeks. tug gently on a leaf: if the cutting stays firm in the compost it will be rooted and can be potted up individually. placed outside in a sheltered spot to harden off and. when it has reached a suitable size. finally planted out in the garden.

Fig. 11 Root Cuttings   Fig. 12 Air Layering

Semi-ripe cuttings

These are taken at the end of summer when the new season's growth has begun to ripen and go woody near the base. Cuttings should be non-flowering and about 10-15cm (4-6in) long. This type of cutting is best for woody-stemmed perennials. Pull the cutting away from the main stem. taking a small flap or 'heel' of old bark at the base (which is why they are sometimes called heel cuttings). Callus forms at this heel. Trim the end of it if it is long or ragged. and remove the leaves as for soft cuttings (*Fig. 10b*). Dip the cut end into hormone rooting powder. Semi-ripe cuttings will root in much cooler conditions than softwood cuttings so there is no need for a propagating unit. they will do fine on the greenhouse staging.

Hardwood cuttings

This type of cutting makes use of fully mature wood of the current year's growth – hardwood cuttings should not be more than one year old. Take the cuttings from late autumn to midwinter during the plant's dormant period. If the sap is still running when the cutting is taken it may dry out. adversely affecting the cambium layer.

Hardwood cuttings are slow to root. so you must have space in your garden to leave them undisturbed for at least one year. Only a small range of plants are suitable for hardwood cuttings: roses are favourites for this treatment (although I have had more success with internodal cuttings). The cuttings should be pencil-thick and about 30–45cm (12–18in) long. but take a cutting longer than you need and then trim it by cutting the top end above a node at a slant to shed rain and cutting the bottom end straight across just below a node. (The different ends also help to identify top and bottom.)

Make a V-shaped trench about 20cm (8in) deep and put a 5cm (2in) layer of sharp sand in the bottom to provide drainage which will help to activate the cambium. You can use hormone rooting powder. but it will need to be of higher strength than for other types of cutting. Put the cuttings into the trench so that

they stand upright. not leaning. and are at a depth of at least two-thirds their length (*Fig. 10c*).

Basal cuttings

Basal cuttings are taken from the new shoots that appear at the base of herbaceous perennials and shrubs in early spring. When the basal stems are a few centimetres long cut them just below a leaf or joint. using a clean. sharp knife. Dip the cut ends into hormone rooting powder and put the cuttings into pots or trays of loose compost. Alternatively. they can be rooted in a cold frame.

Internodal cuttings

These are taken in summer from a new. healthy. non-flowering side shoot. Trim to leave 2.5cm (1in) of stem above and below a leaf node selected for the healthy. fat bud it holds at the junction of the leaf and main stem (*Fig. 10d*). Treat as for a soft cutting. but leave at least one leaf and bud. Pot up the cutting. putting the node below the surface of the compost. Roots will develop at the base of the node.

Division

This method of increasing your stock of a plant entails lifting it from its flowering position during its dormant period and then cutting or pulling it apart to create a number of smaller plant clumps. With age. many herbaceous perennials begin to die out in the middle of the clump but continue to make new growth around the edges. It is from here that you take the new plants. making sure that each one has at least two or three growth points. Use an old but sharp kitchen knife to cut through woody or fibrous root masses. and a pair of garden forks. back to back. to prise apart stringy-rooted clumps like hostas. Before replanting. I usually trim the roots by grasping them in a bunch near the crown of the plant and then cutting away any straggling ends that protrude.

Alternate   Opposite   Whorls

Fig. 13 Leaf Arrangements

Root cuttings

A few herbaceous plants such as oriental poppies are propagated by means of root cuttings. They are taken in late winter or when the plant has been lifted for division. Cut pieces of healthy root about 5–7.5cm (2–3in) long. Cut the bottom end of the root section (the end furthest from the top growth) at a slant to identify which way is up (*Fig. 11*). Put thick roots vertically in pots of compost, lay thin roots horizontally on compost-filled trays. Cover with about 6mm (1/4in) of compost or vermiculite, and stand the containers in a cold frame or cold greenhouse. When new shoots appear the plants can be potted individually.

Runners

An easy way to propagate a number of groundcovering plants is by making cuttings from the new growths that appear at the end of long trailing stems. Saxifrages, ivy, strawberries and mint are a few familiar runner-producing plants. Simply peg the juvenile plant at the end of the runner into a pot of compost; as soon as it roots, the runner can be severed and the baby plant moved to a new home. If you wish to root many runners of one plant, just separate the babies from the parent plant, put them into a tray of compost, water with fungicide solution, cover and set out in a sheltered spot. They will take root in a few weeks.

Layering

This means of propagation is useful for certain woody perennials like rhododendrons, azaleas, gardenias and groundcover plants that root as they cover the ground. Select a branch or stem that can easily be pulled down to the ground. Make a small slit in the bark at the point where the branch touches the ground; it should be far enough from the growing tip for the latter still to be held well above ground when the layering point is firmed into the soil. Dust the wound with rooting powder and peg it down on the soil using a length of bent wire or a clothes peg. Cover with compost, and when the new growth appears, cut the layer from the old plant and pot on until it is strong enough to plant out.

Air layering

This is similar in practice to layering except that the wounded bark is wrapped in a moist medium and the roots develop into this before being potted into compost. Select a healthy, straight semi-ripe side shoot and with a sharp knife make a wound by slicing along the stem towards the growing tip and then lift a narrow tongue of bark (*Fig. 12*). Use a toothpick to hold the flap open and dust the wound with hormone rooting compound.

Wrap the wounded portion in damp sphagnum moss and bind the moss loosely in a plastic bag. Then wrap this in plastic to prevent it drying out, sealing both ends with plant ties. Water the main plant regularly and in several months you should see roots poking through the moss. Sever the shoot from the old plant, cutting cleanly just below the new roots, then pot it up.

The Leaf

The chief function of leaves is food production, for they are the main site of photosynthesis. This is most simply expressed as the process of creating complex chemicals (sugars and oxygen) from simple ones (carbon dioxide and water) using either natural light (sunlight) or artificial light. In photosynthesis the leaf absorbs light and carbon dioxide from the atmosphere and processes them into sugars like glucose, releasing oxygen as a by-product of the chemical changes. Leaves also allow the plants to transpire, shedding excess water to cool the plant.

The three main ways in which leaves are arranged around the stem are shown in Fig. 13. Similarly, there are three main ways

Fig. 14 Leaf Types

Petiole leaf   Sessile leaf   Compound leaf

Opposite Apart from their aesthetic appeal, leaves sustain the life of a plant, provide the energy, and often the means by which it can be reproduced.

Fig. 15 Cross-section to show Leaf Structure

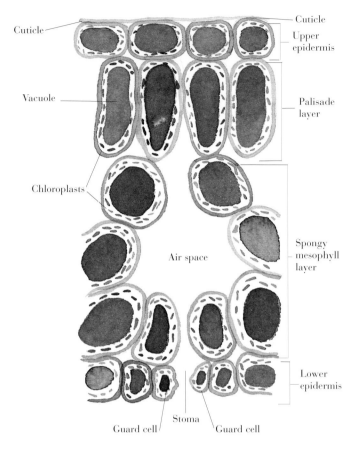

Cuticle

Cuticle
Upper epidermis

Vacuole

Palisade layer

Chloroplasts

Spongy mesophyll layer

Air space

Lower epidermis

Guard cell

Stoma

Guard cell

the pigments which give leaves their colour. The spongy mesophyll are the lungs of the plant, and breathe through the stomata on the lower epidermis of the plant: in respiration, the stomata allow oxygen in and carbon dioxide out, reversing the process during photosynthesis. There are a few stomata on the upper epidermis also. The guard cells either side of the openings also respond to moisture, opening and closing the stomata: in a moist atmosphere the stomata remain open, and in dry heat they shut rapidly. That is why a constant misted atmosphere is desirable in propagation to avoid stressing the food-producing cells within the leaves as the cuttings try to establish roots.

The midribs and veins contain the vascular bundles, and thus the cambium layer needed for propagation.

Leaf blade cuttings

These are used for streptocarpus, sansevieria (mother-in-law's tongue) begonias and Christmas and Easter cactus. Take a healthy mature leaf, place it upside-down on a clean surface and with a sterile sharp knife make small incisions across the main veins, cutting through to the other side (*Fig. 16*). Turn the leaf right-side facing and place it on a tray of moist compost. To make sure that the cuts have contact with the compost, use a few clean pebbles to hold the leaf in place. Put the tray in a propagator: in a matter of weeks, roots will form at the cuts and new plantlets will emerge on the top of the old leaf.

Alternatively, cut the leaf into squares, making sure that a vein runs through the centre of each square. Sections of begonia leaf can be laid flat on the compost while streptocarpus leaf cuttings can be inserted upright to half their depth. There is no need to cut the cactus leaves into pieces: simply detach a segment and put it to half its depth in compost.

in which the leaf is joined by its petiole to the main stem of the plant (*Fig. 14*) to allow the leaf to turn in the direction of the light. Leaves are designed to help the plant make the most of the growing conditions in its native habitat: for example, many tropical rainforest plants grow in low light levels, so the leaves have large, light-gathering surfaces with thick waxy cuticles to help prevent water loss in the hot atmosphere while plants in hot, dry, sunny climates often have tiny leaves, covered in oil glands to help conserve moisture.

The detailed structure of a leaf seen in cross-section through a microscope appears as layers of cells, each layer performing a separate function (*Fig. 15*). The uppermost layer is the cuticle, which gives the leaf resistance to water and fungal diseases. Next is the upper epidermis, made of tightly fitting square cells with a vacuole or reservoir of water in the centre of each cell. When the plant is turgid the vacuoles are fully charged with water, giving the leaf support and helping the plant to retain its shape. Beneath this is the palisade layer, with more closely fitted cells, each with vacuoles at their centres, and containing chloroplasts. This is the site of photosynthetic action. The chloroplasts produce carbon dioxide, moving through the palisade layer towards the transparent epidermal layer to gather light, and also contain

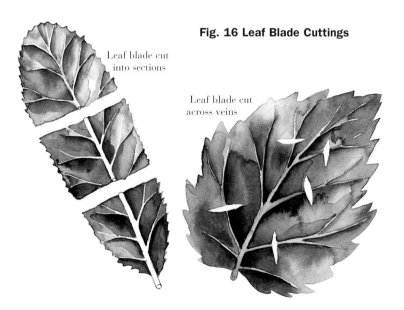

Fig. 16 Leaf Blade Cuttings

Leaf blade cut into sections

Leaf blade cut across veins

Fig. 17 Leaf Petiole Cuttings

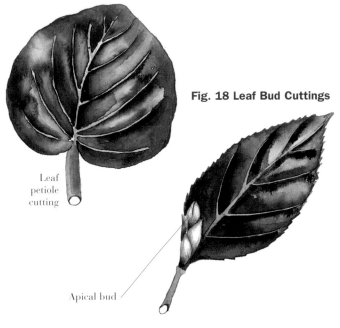

Fig. 18 Leaf Bud Cuttings

Leaf petiole cutting

Apical bud

tained underground units. The two main types of bulb are scaly bulbs such as lilies and tunicate bulbs such as daffodils and snowdrops.

Scaly bulb scales can be used for propagation (*Fig. 19*) remove individual scales from the bulb, insert upright into trays of moist compost and eventually small bulbils will form at the base of each scale. Some lilies also produce tiny bulbils along the flower stem in the leaf axils. Simply take the stem, lay it in a tray of moist compost, cover in a fine layer of moist grit or horticultural vermiculite and the bulbils will develop roots. They can then be detached and grown on before planting out.

When you lift clumps of bulbs or corms you will often see mini bulbs or corms (offsets) crowding around the base (*Fig. 20*). Carefully remove them and set out in a nursery bed to grow on for two years, or until they are large enough to plant out in the garden.

Bulbs produced from these methods will take several years to come to flower, during which time they must be regularly fed and watered.

Fig. 19 Scaly Bulb

Bulblet forming on interior of scale at its base

Leaf petiole cuttings

This method uses the leaf and petiole only. Select a healthy leaf and cut the petiole to about 2.5cm (1in). Insert in the compost at a shallow angle, not upright, taking care that the leaf does not touch the soil (*Fig. 17*). You can put several leaves in one pot. Put the stem in so that it is held. Water with a fungicide solution and put into the propagator, shaded from direct sunlight. This method is most widely used for African violets and many other succulent plants.

Leaf bud cuttings

This is a good method of propagation when there is a shortage of healthy cutting material or the shoots from which cuttings would normally be taken have become etiolated. Leaf buds use only the section of the stem between the tip bud and uppermost leaf; this type of cutting is also sometimes called a tip cutting. Clematis, Virginia creeper, mahonias, camellias and rubber plants are just a few of the plants that respond to this treatment. Cut the stem cleanly just below the leaf node on the uppermost leaf (*Fig. 18*), use hormone rooting powder and insert the cuttings in the compost, several to a pot or tray. Put in a propagating unit.

Bulbs

Bulbs, corms, tubers and rhizomes are in effect small parcels containing all the elements of growth and structure in self-con-

Fig. 20 Tunicate Bulb

Flower bud

Scale leaves

Bulblets forming from axillary buds

THE
PLANT DIRECTORY

THROUGHOUT THIS BOOK I HAVE POINTED OUT HOW important it is to suit the plants to the site. When I first began gardening I tried to grow everything, regardless of whether or not I could provide the conditions for good growth that the plant required. Experience, gained at the cost of countless losses of sometimes expensive plants, has taught me the error of beginner's enthusiasm (although it may have been failure that goaded me on, seeking success). Consequently, the soil and sun conditions required are given for all the plants in this index. The degrees of soil moisture range from dry to well-drained (moisture drains away rapidly), moisture-retentive (moisture remains in the soil but without making it permanently soggy) and wet (permanently soggy). The conditions of light range from full sun to semi-shade and full shade. The combinations of these conditions will determine the temperature of the soil; a dry soil in sun is more likely to be warm than a moisture-retentive soil in sun as the evaporating moisture will help to keep roots cool to some degree.

The shagbark hickory, *Carya ovata*, adds its vibrant yellow tints to the autumn show in the forests of New England, yet a mature tree is just as noteworthy for its peeling ragged bark. *Overleaf left*, flowering cherries, like *Prunus serrulata* 'Shirotae' have rich autumn tints, and the berry-covered spikes of the arum lily, *Zantedeschia aethiopica (overleaf right)*, will also continue the show after flowers have faded.

All soils can be ameliorated to improve their condition, but they cannot be permanently altered. That is why I, for example, don't attempt to grow acid-loving plants on my slightly alkaline soil – I don't want to have to keep digging in peat in an effort to create acid conditions.

The entries are grouped first according to colour and visual interest and then by a loose classification of annuals and perennials, shrubs and climbers and trees. It was difficult to know where to draw the line among the plants I have included. Over the years I have developed a palette of leafy plants which remain firm favourites and have been included in each garden I have made. Some of the plants listed come highly recommended by gardening friends; there are others which I have enjoyed growing in the past, and some which will feature in the future. I'd love to garden in the south-western United States so that I could have a garden full of cacti and succulents, or in Hobart, Tasmania, so that my garden could be filled with as many of the scented native shrubs as I could accumulate – and I long to grow candlebark eucalyptus! But that is what makes gardening such a pleasure, dreaming about what you could grow and will grow. No doubt some of you will discover that one or more of your favourite foliage plants has been ignored (I don't have much time for ornamental conifers, for example, although I know there are some pretty ones about), but I hope I will have introduced some unfamiliar plants instead. Above all, I hope this list will encourage you to begin composing your own plant directory, to go into the garden looking not just at the flower colour, but also taking in the huge variety of leaf shapes, textures and colours, and the equally vibrant variations in shape and habit of bark and berries.

YELLOW, ORANGE, RED & PURPLE

A ground-covering mat of *Ajuga reptans* 'Atropurpurea' is like a spilled bottle of old claret; the colour is best in semi-shade, and makes a perfect backdrop to spring bulbs like grape hyacinths, scillas and buttery yellow primroses. When these flowers fade, the everpurple ajuga foliage remains to support its own show of blue flower spikes.

Semi-shaded or even fully shaded corners can be brightened up with the fresh acid-green spring growth of
Filipendula ulmaria 'Aurea'.

Annuals and perennials

Ajuga reptans is a groundcovering
perennial that has glossy green, long
oval leaves and early-summer spikes of
lilac-blue flowers. 'Atropurpurea' is dark
vinous purple; 'Catlin's Giant' has large,
brownish-purple leaves; 'Burgundy
Glow' has cream-edged rose and purple
colouring; 'Multicolor' has bronze-green
leaves splashed with pink and white and
'Variegata' has pale green leaves
blotched with cream. Propagate from
rooted runners. It likes moisture-
retentive soil in semi-shade.

Cordyline australis is one of the garden
designer's favourite architectural plants,
popularly used as a specimen plant in
urns and formal containers or else as a
sort of living sculpture in borders and
vistas. In cold zones give it winter
protection or put it under glass. An
evergreen perennial, it comes in a range
of warm tints; the names 'Sundance',
'Torbay Dazzler' and 'Torbay Red' give
some idea of the colours. It requires well-
drained soil in sun.

Filipendula ulmaria **'Aurea'** is the
brightest tinted form of meadowsweet;

the palmate leaves are acid green and
the plant makes a bright mound in a
shady corner of the springtime garden.
The colour deepens as the flower stalks
appear in midsummer. Propagate by
division. A hardy perennial, it requires
moisture-retentive soil in semi-shade.

Geranium sessiliflorum **'Nigricans'** is a
good ground-hugging geranium with
thumbnail-sized brown leaves sprinkled
over in midsummer with small white
flowers. It self-sows admirably so will
soon colonize, especially if grown in
gravel. It mingles beautifully with brown

Humulus lupulus 'Aureus' *(left)* is the golden-leaved hop, a perennial climber that will quickly cover trellis or wire supports. It can be grown through trees and evergreens, but is quite aggressive so should be thinned when the shoots first begin to climb. The black-leaved lily turf, *Ophiopogon planiscapus* 'Nigrescens' *(right)*, is among the plants which will provide the darkest foliage tints year-round; its dwarf cousin *O. japonicus* 'Minor' makes a good substitute for grass turf in hot arid conditions, and can be used to edge paving.

grasses like *Carex comans* bronze form or blue *Festuca glauca*. Propagate from cuttings taken in summer. It is an extremely easy perennial, preferring well-drained soil in sun and even tolerating drought conditions.

Houttuynia cordata 'Chameleon' is a charming water's edge groundcover with heart-shaped leaves blotched with red and cream; the variegation is improved if the plant gets a few hours of sun each day. It is quite vigorous and will quickly carpet a boggy bank, carrying little white starry flowers in summer.

Propagate by division in spring. This hardy perennial likes moisture-retentive soil in sun or semi-shade.

Humulus lupulus 'Aureus' is the golden hop, with the same vigorous climbing habit of the species but with bright canary-yellow juvenile foliage, becoming gradually greener with age. Propagate from basal cuttings or by division. This perennial climber likes well-drained soil in semi-shade.

Lysimachia nummularia 'Aurea' (moneywort, creeping jenny) A vigorous,

evergreen groundcover plant with round yellow leaves. Propagate by division in spring; plant in a moisture-retentive soil in semi-shade.

Milium effusum 'Aureum' (Bowles's golden grass) This has the most satisfyingly canary-yellow leaves, long, broad and rather limp, and in midsummer similarly coloured erect stems topped by elegant open panicles of dainty flowers. It spreads slowly by underground rhizomes and also seeds itself around, coming true from seed; a colony makes pools of sunlight in a woodland planting.

Lysimachia nummularia 'Aurea' *(left)* rapidly makes a tightly woven blanket of small leaves and can be clipped back to keep it in check. *Phormium tenax (right)* offers a wide colour range in its strap-like leaves and being tall in stature makes a good feature plant.

It can also be propagated by division. It likes moisture-retentive soil in shade.

***Ophiopogon planiscapus* 'Nigrescens'** This grass-like perennial is a real curiosity for the squid's-ink blackness of its curving strap-like leaves. It makes a good companion for blue-flowered plants and brown and rust-coloured foliage plants. Propagate from the creeping rhizomes and plant in a well-drained soil in sun or semi-shade.

***Origanum vulgare* 'Aureum'** is the golden-leaved form of the herb marjoram, a creeping groundcover that makes a vivid yellow carpet of tiny round leaves topped by a thin dusting of pale mauve flowers in summer. Propagate by division. This hardy perennial likes a well-drained soil in sun.

Perilla frutescens is an oriental herb known in the West as the 'beefsteak plant' (use it in salads or stir-fries as you would spinach). The dark purple-black leaves and stems make it a good 'dot' plant in bedding schemes, and the rough seersucker surface of the glossy leaves seems to reflect light to an extent unusual in a dark foliage plant. This is a half-hardy annual; raise from seed sown under glass in early spring for planting out after frosts, or else sow in succession in the vegetable garden when the soil has warmed. It likes well-drained soil in sun.

Phormium The Purpureum group of *P. tenax* offer a good bronze-purple colour and strong vertical accent from the stiff sword-like leaves. There are a number of cultivars with other tints of rose, cream, verdigris and mauve, including *P. cookianum* ssp. *hookeri* 'Cream Delight' and 'Tricolor', *P. tenax* 'Variegatum'

The smoke bush *Cotinus coggygria (left)*, has many cultivars each with its own distinctive tint of purple-red. Hard pruning after flowering will encourage larger leaves, but left alone, it will make a large open shrub that works well in a mixed border with old shrub roses.

are all good forms of the smoke bush, so called for the billowing, hazy effect of the flowerheads. 'Royal Purple' has the darkest colouring. The best foliage is produced on plants that are coppiced in late autumn or winter. *C. obovatus*, the American smoke tree, is taller growing and colours in autumn from plum-purple to hot gold and russet red. Propagate by semi-ripe cuttings in late summer and plant these medium-sized shrubs in moisture-retentive soil in sun.

Gleditsia triacanthos (honey locust) Grow the cultivar 'Sunburst' for its

bright yellow pinnate leaves that change gradually to soft green as they age. It is a small deciduous tree but is best grown as a large shrub by pruning hard each winter after leaf fall to encourage a vivid display. The wood is quite brittle, and keeping it low will help to avoid wind damage. It likes a well-drained soil in full sun, will grow on chalk and can withstand periods of drought.

Nandina domestica Semi-evergreen small shrub with leaves tinged red and purple in spring and autumn. Propagate from semi-ripe cuttings in late summer.

Requires a sheltered position and well-drained soil.

Trees

***Catalpa bignonioides* 'Aurea'** (Indian bean tree) Big, broad, heart-shaped leaves and bold trusses of outsize snapdragon-like flowers followed by 30cm (12in) long pendent 'beans' make this a dramatic large specimen tree. The brightness of the yellow deciduous leaves (up to 20cm [8in] long and wide) just serves to emphasize its presence. It will grow in any soil in sun.

The golden-leaved Indian bean tree, *Catalpa bignonioides* 'Aurea' *(centre)*, makes a stunning specimen tree in a large garden. Everything about the tree is 'big' – from the flower candelabras to the pendent 'bean' seedpods, and the large leaves which give it a coarse, eye-catching texture. *Nandina domestica (right)*, creates thickets in the forest understorey and so makes a good medium-height filler plant beneath trees and between taller growing shrubs.

Cercis canadensis (Judas tree) is a lovely addition to the springtime garden, underplanted with daffodils or bluebells: the pink flowers nestle amid the pink-tinged heart-shaped leaves, which take on a more greenish cast as they age. The foliage of *C. c.* 'Forest Pansy' colours purple in the autumn, and in both forms the fallen leaves have an unmistakable warm scent of candy floss. It is a small deciduous tree that likes moist soil (preferably acid) in sun.

Fagus sylvatica **'Rohanii'** (purple fern-leaf beech) has deeply laciniate leaves,

while *F. s.* 'Purpurea Pendula' offers purple foliage and an attractive weeping habit of growth. Unless you appreciate looming dark masses, I recommend keeping purple-leaved subjects to a supporting role in the garden and working them in among brighter-coloured trees. These are large deciduous trees that will grow in any soil in sun.

Prunus cerasifera **'Pissardii'** (syn. *P. c.* 'Atropurpurea') Even though this is a paler purple than the inky 'Nigra' it still has a rather glum effect. However, teamed with some incendiary reds and

oranges, its sombre effect can be relieved. It is a medium-sized deciduous tree that likes well-drained soil in sun and does well on chalk soils.

Robinia pseudoacacia **'Frisia'** is the rich yellow-leaved form of the black locust: the deciduous leaves are pinnate, giving the tree a fluffy prettiness. The colour is good from spring through to late autumn, making this a valuable brightener for the garden. Although it is small it requires careful positioning as it is thorny. It will grow in any soil in sun and tolerates dry conditions.

GREEN

Since Classical times, the glossy acanthus leaf has served as architectural ornament; think of it in this context
when placing *Acanthus mollis* in the garden.

The feather-like fronds of *Adiantum pedatum (left)* are strikingly marked by the shiny black stalks that carry each delicate leaflet or pinnule: it grows easily in any moist. humus-rich soil in shade. *Astilboides tabularis (right)* is another moist-shade lover. but its leaves are more substantial. making a good groundcover among shade-loving spring flowers.

Annuals and perennials

Acanthus **spp.** (bear's breeches)
A hardy perennial. semi-evergreen in sheltered areas. with large leathery leaves and architectural flower spikes. *A. mollis*'s large mid-green leaves have a heart-shaped base: *A. spinosa*'s leaves are finely cut and spiny. Propagate by root cuttings in late autumn/winter or by seed. Position in well-drained soil in sun or semi-shade.

Adiantum venustum is a deciduous perennial fern that naturalizes in damp shady corners in mild regions. It has lacy foliage: *A. pedatum* is a hardy. woodland fern. growing in the Aleutian Islands and the cool moist gardens of North America and Europe. Propagate from divisions taken in spring. It prefers acid soil in semi-shade.

Aruncus dioicus **'Kneiffii'** makes a clump of the finest. laciest foliage of any perennial: each leaf is deeply cut. with the edges serrated and coloured a mild green. It has a stiff. branching habit and in midsummer is topped by a frothy plume of starry white flowers. Propagate by division in autumn. Position in well-drained soil in sun or semi-shade.

Asplenium scolopendrium (syn. *Phyllitis scolopendrium*) This is the common woodland hart's tongue fern. of which there are numerous forms: the Crispum group offers dainty plants with attractively crinkled edges to the tongue-shaped leaves. Propagate by division of the crown in spring and plant in moist. chalky soil in semi-shade.

Astilboides tabularis is a hardy perennial with bright green umbrella-

Gardeners in temperate climates are hard pushed for mammoth-leaved plants, but *Gunnera manicata* fits the bill perfectly: well-grown in a water's edge site, or else in humus-rich, retentive soil it will make a clump easily 2.5m (8ft) tall. The species *G. chilensis*, found as far south as Patagonia, is a degree or two hardier but still appreciates heavy winter mulching.

shaped leaves. Propagate by division of rhizomes in spring. Requires moist soil in semi-shade.

Gunnera manicata is probably one of the greatest glories of water's edge planting: the leaves on a mature plant can be as much as 1.5m (5ft) across – and this plant is a herbaceous perennial! It is not entirely frost hardy, so in cold zones it should be heavily mulched during winter by folding the fading leaves over the crown and then covering in a thick layer of straw or other mulch material. This plant requires moist soil

in sun or semi-shade. Propagate by division of new crowns in spring.

Lysichiton camtschatcensis and **L. americanus** are bog or water plants which have white or yellow spathes respectively wrapped around the poker of insignificant flowers: these appear in early spring and are then followed by long, broadly tapering leaves glossy in texture and emerald green in colour. Don't be put off by the common name of skunk cabbage – they are real stunners for the stream or water garden. Propagate by division in spring. These

are hardy perennials that need wet soil in sun or semi-shade.

Matteuccia struthiopteris, commonly known as ostrich fern, has its erect, bright green fronds arranged like a shuttlecock, which is its other alias. Propagate by division of the rhizomatous root in spring. This deciduous fern requires moist soil in semi-shade.

Musa basjoo (banana) and **M. acuminata** (blood banana) are admirable foliage plants where a pronounced exotic effect is desired.

Matteuccia struthiopteris revels in damp shady or semi-shaded places and is especially well-suited to bog garden plantings where the constant level of moisture and humid conditions are just to its liking. In such a spot it can be invasive, but it is worth tolerating this for the soft visual effect of the feathery fronds. Try to plant it so that the low evening light will illuminate the foliage for a brief, brilliant moment.

They are tropical plants, so you must have the space and warmth to accommodate them if you live anywhere north of the Equator – and the strength to move them, as they can grow to quite a size. The blood banana gets its name for the wine-red colouring of the central rib and stem of the long, flat, oval leaves; it looks terrific planted with canna lilies and the coppery-red *Ricinus communis (see page 102)*. These perennials require a sunny position, frequent feeding during the growing period and deeply dug moisture-retentive soil, enriched with plenty of organic matter, to do well.

Polystichum setiferum (soft shield fern) has long feathery evergreen fronds that curve gently at the tips. 'Divisilobum Densum' has a curious fuzzy look about it because of the finely divided, densely crowded fronds: the colour is a pleasing soft green and the midrib caramel brown. Propagate by division of the rhizomes. It requires moisture-retentive soil in semi-shade.

Stipa spp. This genus of mainly perennial clump-forming grasses has about 300 species, of which there is space here only to mention those that are in my opinion the best. *S. arundinacea*, a native of Australia and New Zealand, makes a 0.9–1.2m (3–4ft) tall clump of slender arching leaves that move with sinuous grace in the slightest breeze and take on a golden-russet glow in late autumn. In late summer the flowers form in loose open panicles that create a fine film above the steadily reddening foliage. *S. gigantea* is widely available and deserves its popularity for the erect 1.5m (5ft) tall flowering stems that sway above the grassy hummocks of mid-green narrow leaves. These inflorescences appear in early summer

Used in a pool-side planting, the glimmering leaves of *Zantedeschia aethiopica* 'Crowborough' echo the glistening surface of the water. Although it likes being planted in water, it will grow in any moisture-retentive soil. This form is hardy enough to grow outdoors year-round even in cool gardens, but nevertheless will benefit from having its rhizomatous roots deeply mulched.

and retain their beauty over a long season: the seed spikes become increasingly golden brown, and if positioned to catch the sun will glisten in the breeze. *S. tenuissima* has what is probably the finest foliage and flowers among the grasses: each leaf and flower stem is as slender as silken thread and as the seedheads ripen the plant takes on a soft wheaten glow. It only reaches about 45cm (18in) and looks splendid grown with the daisy-flowered *Anthemis* 'E. C. Buxton' as seen in Beth Chatto's superb gravel garden in Essex, England. Propagate by division in the spring or

by seed sown when ripe at the end of summer. They require well-drained soil in sun.

Veratrum nigrum is a hardy perennial better known for the curious pleating of its young foliage than for the tall, erect flower spikes bearing unusual chocolate-coloured blooms. As the broad, tapering leaves begin to unfurl in early summer they have the crumpled delicacy of the fabled silken Fortuny textiles, with each frond deeply pleated. They look their best then, as the foliage begins to lose the pronounced texturing as it ages. A

native of the woodland edge, this plant can be propagated by division of the crowns in early spring or from self-sown seedlings, though it takes quite a few years for seedlings to develop to a moveable size. It likes moisture-retentive soil in semi-shade.

Zantedeschia aethiopica **'Crowborough'** (arum lily) A hardier form of this half-hardy perennial with mid- to deep green, glossy arrow-shaped leaves. Propagate by offsets in winter. Plant in moisture-retentive soil in sun or semi-shade.

The evergreen ivy is a perennial favourite and *Hedera helix* 'Green Ripple' *(centre)*, with its deeply lobed and clearly veined leaves, is one of the more striking green-leaved sorts: it can be grown as a groundcover in woodland gardens or as a wall-trained plant. *Ilex cornuta* 'Burfordii' *(right)* has only a single spine at the tip of each shiny oval leaf, making it rather more garden-friendly than some – a useful feature in a garden where children play.

Shrubs and climbers

Eriobotrya japonica (loquat) This large deciduous shrub bears curious pear-shaped yellow fruit, though these only appear if there is enough summer heat to encourage the heavily scented flowers to emerge. However, the long, tapering, leathery leaves make this an attractive shrub which looks best against a wall. Propagate from semi-ripe cuttings in late summer and grow in any soil in sun.

Hedera helix **vars** 'Green Ripple' is named for the rippling mid- to light green of its strongly veined leaves and valued for its branching habit. 'Conglomerata' is one of the most curious of the small-leaved evergreen ivies, known for its rigidly erect habit of growth and the way the leaves are held stiffly in evenly spaced parallel ranks along the stems. Increase from cuttings in late summer and plant in moisture-retentive soil in semi-shade.

Hydrangea sargentiana The leaves, stems and flowerheads of this not entirely hardy hydrangea are covered in downy hairs, giving the whole shrub a foggy, soft-focus look. Because of its tenderness, it is best given wall protection. It makes a tall shrub and should be planted in moisture-retentive soil in semi-shade.

Ilex **spp.** Of the evergreen shrubs, the hollies, with their light-reflecting glossy leaves, are real attention-getters. Depending on the cultivar, the berries range in colour from deep red to bright yellow; you must plant a male and female to have berries. There are dozens of species and named cultivars to choose from: *I. cornuta* 'Burfordii' is a dense,

Magnolia grandiflora (above), with its fleshy flowers and sturdy leathery leaves, has a demanding presence and is often used as a specimen tree in formal, Italianate gardens. But no tree surpasses *Cupressus sempervirens (opposite)* for instantly summoning up visions of Mediterranean gardens. It is the strongest vertical element in the fabled landscapes of Classical and Renaissance gardens, and is widely used today, as here in the south of France at La Casella to create formal avenues and vistas.

compact female form with entire or spiny leaves. *I. aquifolium* 'Green Pillar' is an erect, narrow female form with dark green spiny leaves. 'Myrtifolia' is a male shrub with small dark green leaves and variable spining while 'Pyramidalis' has green stems and bright green slightly spiny leaves. Increase by soft-wood cuttings in late summer. Any soil in sun or shade will suffice.

Magnolia grandiflora Fabled for its vast creamy white waxy flowers and heady perfume, this large tree has ever-green foliage quite as striking as the blooms. Large, glossy dark green ovals (often with reddish-brown felt beneath) provide a perfect setting for the white flowers; in warm zones it grows happily as a tree (seeing rows of young trees covered in shining leaves and perfect flowers lined out in Italian nurseries at Pistoia is a sight for sore eyes) but in colder regions it is best trained as a large shrub against a warm wall. 'Undulata' has distinctly veined leaves with wavy margins that are glossy green above and green beneath even when immature. These plants require well-drained soil in sun and are tolerant of lime, even over chalk, provided there is a good depth of loam.

Trees

Alnus glutinosa 'Imperialis' is the most distinguished member of the alders. A medium-sized deciduous tree with very finely cut leaves, it should perhaps be helped with a little pruning to take a more stately posture than it typically would; many trees respond well to this sort of treatment. Yellow catkins add to its charms in early spring. It will thrive in any soil in sun or semi-shade.

The use of tender exotics in cool temperate gardens expands the range of foliage you can use but also increases the challenge; the Australian native man fern, *Dicksonia antarctica (left)*, is one such plant, its fibrous trunk and long fronds evoking the primeval jungle. With fig trees like *Ficus carica (above)*, however, the warm spicy scent of the foliage and large leather leaves designed to withstand heat and drought bring to mind sunny Mediterranean gardens.

Azara microphylla Tiny round dark green leaves are neatly arrayed along the fanned-out branches of this large evergreen shrub or small tree, most often grown as a wall-trained specimen. In the earliest days of spring tiny lily-vanilla-scented flowers nestle in the leaf axils, cheering up a cold grey border. It will grow in any soil in sun or semi-shade.

Cupressus sempervirens (Italian cypress) This is one of the most evocative plants I know, calling to mind the sensual pleasures of Tuscan gardens and warm Italian nights scented with

lime flowers and loud with crickets. In cold gardens these statuesque evergreens are not dependably hardy, but they will be happy enough in containers. They grow to a great age and height in the right conditions, becoming increasingly bare at the base as they mature. Plant in well-drained soil in sun.

Dicksonia antarctica is the Australian man fern, so called because it is the size of a man in its native habitat, though it can grow to as much as 10m (30ft). It has a mysterious primeval aura, and its presence in a garden adds a definite

touch of class. It is not fully hardy, so will need protection in all but the mildest gardens. The deeply divided evergreen fronds spring from the top of the stubby trunk, which is covered in a sort of coconut-fibre hairiness. As the fronds fade they droop down, wrapping themselves around the trunk. Although it is hard to resist tidying them up, these should be left to provide a sort of mulch protection around the trunk, helping it to conserve moisture and endure the cold. In dry spells it is necessary to mist the fern on a regular basis. It requires moisture-retentive soil in semi-shade.

The groundcovering evergreen branches of *Juniperus communis* 'Repanda' *(left)* serve as a living mulch in woodland gardens; it is one of the most popular junipers and is widely grown. Portugese laurel, *Prunus lusitanica (right)*, enjoys similar popularity and, with its red leaf stems and small curved leaves, is preferable to the coarser cherry laurel, *P. laurocerasus*.

***Fagus sylvatica* 'Aspleniifolia'** (fern-leaf beech) is even more lovely than the common beech, with which it shares a languid drooping habit and soft autumn colouring. The deeply cut leaves give this large deciduous tree special presence, so use it as a feature plant. It will grow in any soil in sun.

Ficus carica The fig is a curiously unruly plant: it is most often seen growing against a warm wall with its feet encased in concrete-sided pits to try to control its growth by restricting root development (a method which in my

garden has failed completely). However, I have seen it growing elegantly in a small grove of a dozen trees, neatly pruned to uniform mop-headed shapes. The large, leathery, deeply lobed deciduous leaves have an equally curious scent you either love or hate. The drooping branches will root where they touch the ground, or new plants can be raised from semi-ripe cuttings in late summer. It likes well-drained soil in sun.

Juniperus spp. and cultivars

Evergreens give backbone to a garden, and none more so than the junipers,

which range from tall-growing trees to shrubs or dwarf specimens for rockery gardens. Generally speaking they are a slow-growing group of trees with the exception of the widely available *J. scopulorum* 'Skyrocket', which starts off with a trim conical shape, but as it ages begins to lean and open up. For pencil shapes, *J. communis* offers several good cultivars: 'Hibernica' is very popular, as is the form *suecica*, and the really slow grower, 'Compressa'; *J. chinensis* 'Columnaris Glauca' makes a small vertical tree. For low-spreading shapes, *J. communis* 'Hornibrookii' is

Grey-leaved plants provide some of the finest textures in the garden: *Sedum spectabile* 'Autumn Joy' *(left)* has tight rosettes of slightly frilled fleshy leaves while the felted texture of *Stachys byzantina (right)* adds soft radiance to underplantings amid spring-flowering shrubs and early perennials.

fashioned roses or as a punctuation point in the border. In late summer it will produce tall flowering stalks bearing the artichoke-shaped flowers tipped with rich mauve bristles. Do not position where the sharp spines which sometimes appear on the leaf serrations will be a danger. Propagate from offsets in spring. A herbaceous perennial, it requires well-drained soil in sun; protect at the base with a mulch in cold zones.

Helleborus × sternii The leathery pedate leaves of hellebores are evergreen and make pleasing rounded mounds,

providing good backgrounds to later-flowering plants. This form has large, open leaf fronds and each individual leaf is prettily netted over with silver veins against a pale green ground, giving the plant an attractive silvery sheen. It requires well-drained soil in sun.

Lychnis coronaria is a traditional cottage-garden hardy perennial best known for the fuchsia-pink flowers that appear in midsummer. However, throughout spring and early summer it is a spreading clump of narrow felted silvery-grey leaves, gradually taking on

height to about 45cm (18in), turning the plant into a useful vertical accent. Propagate from seed. It prefers sun to shade and will grow in any soil.

Sedum spp. *S. spectabile* is the most common of the succulent sedum tribe, making a clump of oval leaves and becoming a rounded mass of flowering stalks, 45cm (18in) tall by midsummer. 'Autumn Joy' carries the typical grey-green leaves; *S. caucasicum* makes a sprawling clump of stems bearing grey-green leaves shaped like clam shells; *S. ruprechtii* has a similar sharply defined

The lanceolate leaves of *Elaeagnus angustifolia (left)* are cut from fine silver plate while the stems are dipped in bronze, and the scented golden flowers become amber beads, or so it would seem. The oleaster is a common shrub in shelter belt plantings, particularly in seaside gardens. The tender shrub *Melianthus major (right)* makes a strong feature plant, useful in container planting schemes.

character and the leaves take on a purple tinge as the summer ends. Propagate these herbaceous perennials by division in autumn and plant in dry soil in sun.

Stachys byzantina (lamb's ears) A half-hardy groundcovering perennial with woolly, felted grey leaves. 'Silver Carpet' is a non-flowering variety. Propagate by division from autumn to spring. Plant in a well-drained soil in sun or semi-shade.

Verbascum olympicum (giant mullein) is a short-lived perennial that is most

often grown as a biennial. It sows itself freely around the garden, so you will never be without its great rosettes of heavily felted silvery grey leaves. *V. bombyciferum* is perhaps a whiter shade of pale grey. Propagate from seed sown in the summer to flower the following year. They like a well-drained soil in sun.

Shrubs and climbers

Elaeagnus angustifolia (oleaster) Deciduous shrub or small tree with silver willow-like leaves. Propagate

from semi-ripe cuttings. Plant in a well-drained soil in sun or shade.

Melianthus major The large pinnate fronds of this handsome small shrub have a curious chocolatey smell when bruised; an acquired taste for some. It is not hardy, so in cold climates must be overwintered under glass. In summer it has long, tapering racemes of glossy, bead-like flowers, but the foliage is the thing, and gives a distinctly tropical look in a border planting. Propagate from basal cuttings in late summer and plant in a well-drained soil in sun.

Cryptomeria japonica 'Globosa Nana' *(above)* is just one of the several autumn-colouring evergreens this genus provides, contributing purple, bronze and dark red tints to the garden. *Picea pungens* 'Koster Prostrate' *(below)* is, however, a dependable glaucous blue-grey, and the stiff finger-like branches give the shrub an intriguing visual texture.

Perovskia atriplicifolia (Russian sage) is one of the finest grey plants in the late summer garden with silvery-white stems covered in minuscule flowers making clouds of azure blue above the finely cut, ghostly pale foliage. 'Blue Spire' and the lavender-tinted 'Superba' are cultivars to look for. The scent is like sage with a hint of mothballs. Propagate this deciduous subshrub from semi-ripe cuttings in late summer and plant in a well-drained soil in sun.

Rosa rubrifolia has russet-red arching stems and red-tinged grey foliage against which the single flowers, coloured pale rose madder, show up wonderfully. The flowers are followed by clusters of glossy ruby-red hips that last well into winter. Self-sown seedlings will appear, and it can also be increased from semi-ripe cuttings taken in summer. It makes a medium-sized shrub that will thrive in any soil in sun.

Salix lanata is called woolly willow on account of the exceptional caterpillar-like catkins that cover this low spreading shrub in spring. The stubby little rounded leaves also have a silvery bloom. It roots easily from cuttings taken in late summer; give it a moisture-retentive soil in sun.

Salvia officinalis '**Crispa**' The leaves of this decorative form of common sage are more rounded than the species and the edges are crimped, causing the leaves to curl and crinkle. It makes a pleasing low-spreading grey mound. *S. o.* 'Purpurascens' (purple-leaved sage) has a good inky tinge to the grey-green leaves. Propagate by cuttings in late summer. This hardy evergreen shrub prefers well-drained soil in sun.

Trees take their weeping habits from the depth of the angle where branch meets trunk, as can be seen in the weeping *Pyrus salicifolia (below)*. However, the drooping tassels of the needle clusters on the Bhutan pine, *Pinus wallichiana (above)*, contribute the weeping effect to this graceful evergreen.

***Thymus* spp. and cultivars** are the sweetest-smelling groundcovers. *T. pseudolanuginosus*'s tiny leaves are covered in fine silver hairs. To keep a dense mat of foliage, clip the plants after flowering. Increase from rooted pieces lifted in autumn or spring: these mostly hardy plants like well-drained soil in sun.

Trees

Cryptomeria japonica **'Globosa Nana'** A small evergreen shrub with a rounded habit. The leaves turn bronze in winter. Plant in a well-drained soil in sun or partial shade. Propagate by semi-ripe cuttings.

Picea pungens glauca The neat conical habit and uniformly spaced spreading branches of this glaucous evergreen make a terrific feature in the garden but it does need space to do it justice: if you lack that, 'Koster' or 'Koster Prostrate' are smaller-growing with the same colouring. Plant in a well-drained soil in sun or semi-shade.

Pinus wallichiana (Bhutan pine) A large evergreen tree with a weeping appearance and long, graceful, pendulous needles. Plant in a well-drained soil in sun.

Pyrus salicifolia **'Pendula'** is one of the ornamental pears. A small tree, it is grown for the graceful, willow-like silver leaves and its pleasing weeping habit. It benefits from selective pruning and training to help it attain a good shape. *P. calleryana* 'Chanticleer' and *P. c.* 'Bradford' provide brilliant autumn colouring in shades of purple and red respectively. Plant in a well-drained soil in sun.

Among the many hostas that have blue-green colouring, *H. sieboldiana* var. *elegans (left)* is one of the most desirable: the broad flat expanse of its waxy heart-shaped leaves makes an excellent foil to finer-textured foliage plants like the ground-hugging evergreen *Abies procera* 'Glauca Prostrata' *(right)* which has a similar languid colouring.

Helictotrichon sempervirens Next to *Elymus*, this does stand out as one of the duck-eggiest blues in the plant world. It makes a nicely shaped spiky hummock, topped in midsummer by erect stems carrying arching panicles of flowers that fade to a satisfying sandy brown. Propagate by division in spring. Plant in dry soil in the sun and remove faded leaves and flower stems in early spring.

Hosta species and cultivars range in size from tiny groundcovers to clump-forming specimens with an eventual girth of 1.5m (5ft), such as *Hosta sieboldiana* var. *elegans* which has huge deeply puckered silvery blue leaves. Other recommended blue cultivars are 'Big Daddy' with nearly round cupped leaves of chalky glaucous blue and 'Hadspen Blue' with heart-shaped, smooth, thick blue leaves. Use hostas in bold masses or as feature plants or grown in containers. Propagate by division. These herbaceous perennials, native to the forests of Japan and the Far East, appreciate dappled shade and moist soils, although some are tolerant of sun and dry spells, particularly in cool climates. Slugs and snails will disfigure the leaves.

Koeleria vallesiana This perennial grass does well on chalky soil, making a mound of narrow blue-green leaves from which the erect flower stems emerge in midsummer. In all it grows to about 45cm (18in). Divide in the spring. Any soil in sun will be acceptable.

Shrubs and climbers

Abies spp. *A. procera* 'Glauca Prostrata' is a low bush with spreading branches and blue-green glaucous leaves. *A. concolor* 'Compacta' (syn. *A. c.* 'Glauca Compacta') is a small 'blue' conifer with

Lacy-leaved rue is an excellent filler plant in the border among traditional perennials and old shrub roses; 'Jackman's Blue' *(left)* has the best blue colouring, and there is also a cream variegated sort, 'Variegata'. Blue-green foliage is popular among flower arrangers for infilling between cut blooms, and *Eucalyptus cordata (right)* is highly favoured by florists.

a graceful spreading habit and slow growth. It likes a moisture-retentive (preferably acid) soil in sun.

Ruta graveolens is the familiar shrubby herb commonly known as rue. On a sunny day the crushed leaves, which have an astringent pungency, can cause your skin to blister badly, so take care when clipping and tidying. 'Jackman's Blue' has the best-coloured glaucous blue-green foliage. Cut back hard each spring to keep shapely. Propagate by semi-ripe cuttings in summer and plant in well-drained soil in sun.

Trees

Eucalyptus **spp.** One of the most elegant compositions I have ever seen was a burned-out stand of acacia and eucalyptus trees regenerating, with the pastel tints of grey and pink from the gum trees and buttery yellow from the fragrant flowers of the acacia combining beautifully. *E. cordata* (silver gum) is a small tree with silver-grey leaves and an attractive white bark with green or purplish patches. *E. nicholii* (Nichol's willow-leaf peppermint gum) has purple-tinged leaves and a weeping form; *E. perriniana* is the

spinning gum, so called because the mature leaves break from the stem and then spin around it in the wind; *E. pulverulenta* has leaves powdered with grey 'snow'; and *E. risdonii* (Risdon peppermint) has stems covered in a downy white bloom, as does *E. morrisbyi* (Morrisby's gum), which also has graceful lanceolate foliage. Seed from temperate zone parents will yield trees better adapted to cooler winter conditions than those raised from seed collected in Australia. Hard pruning will give the best foliage but will destroy the slender form. They require well-drained soil in sun.

YELLOW-VARIEGATED

Astrantia major 'Sunningdale Variegated', with well-defined markings on its deeply lobed leaves, is one of the better herbaceous perennials valued for their foliage. However, as with many variegated hardy plants, the flowers have considerably less impact than the leaves.

Tender perennials, for example canna lilies, generally have vibrant flowers supported by equally stunning foliage. Orange-flowered *Canna* 'Striata', with its broad oval leaves boldly striped in green and gold, is a popular plant, while the red-flowered 'Lucifer' has dark burgundy-purple foliage.

Annuals and perennials

***Astrantia major* 'Sunningdale Variegated'** This clump-forming hardy perennial is strongly variegated and makes a good feature plant. Propagate by division in spring. Plant in any soil in sun or shade.

***Canna* 'Striata'** A tender perennial with flamboyant foliage, this plant requires a sunny position and a rich well-drained soil. In winter, store in damp peat away from frost. Propagate by division of rhizomes in spring.

***Carex reticulosa* 'Aurea'** Each blade of this vibrant perennial grass is like a ray of watery sunshine: *C. elata* 'Bowles' Golden' is a deeper yellow, edged in emeralds; 'Knightshayes' has the same radiance but without the green edging to each leaf. Propagate from division of rhizomatous roots or from seed and plant in moist soil in semi-shade.

Carex morrowii The bright bundles of variegated foliage are like spotlights in a garden scheme, highlighting interesting corners or illuminating dark ones. A perennial grass only about 15cm (6in) tall, it is most easily increased by division in spring. It likes a moisture-retentive soil in semi-shade.

Hakonechloa macra is a distinctive little perennial grass increasing slowly by its rhizomatous roots to make thickets of arching leaves: there are several variegated cultivars, but the most vigorous and most often seen is 'Aureola', which is very heavily yellow-variegated and showy. As winter approaches, the tips of the leaves become tinged brownish-red. Increase by division in spring and plant in moisture-retentive soil in semi-shade.

Vinca major 'Variegata' *(left)* is a vigorous groundcovering evergreen excellent to use beneath trees and shrubs, but it is too strong for mixed perennial plantings, for which you could use *V. minor* 'Variegata', a smaller, more refined version to partner spring flowers. *Elaeagnus × ebbengei* 'Limelight' *(right)* is a reliable provider of winter interest.

***Molina caerulea* spp. *caerulea* 'Variegata'** This popular perennial grass forms dense tussocks of creamy-white-variegated leaves; *M. c.* ssp. *arundinacea* 'Bergfreund' has bright yellow autumn colouring; *M. c.* ssp. *arundinacea* 'Windspiel' ('Windplay') should, as the name suggests, be planted where the breeze can put it in motion. It is easy to propagate by division in the spring. Plant in moisture-retentive soil in sun.

***Thymus* spp.** and cultivars include some of the best mat-forming yellow-variegated groundcovers, such as *T. caespititius* 'Aureus' and *T. c.* 'Doone Valley', which is particularly bold in its glossy little dark green leaves, heavily marked with yellow. It roots as it spreads so is very easy to propagate. Thyme is a hardy plant that likes well-drained soil in sun.

***Vinca major* 'Variegata'** is the yellow-variegated form of the common periwinkle. This is an evergreen ground-cover that spreads by runners which root where they touch the ground. The leaves are glossy and heavily marked with yellow; used in a shady woodland setting it will look like pools of sunlight. Propagate from rooted runners. It will grow in any soil in sun or semi-shade.

Shrubs and climbers

***Elaeagnus* × *ebbengei* 'Limelight'** This is a large evergreen shrub with a spreading habit. Its leathery green leaves have a central splash of gold or pale green. Alternatively the leaf margins of 'Gilt Edge' are splashed with gold. Propagate from semi-ripe cuttings. Plant in a well-drained soil in sun.

Variegated evergreen plants make good focal points in the garden and also give permanence to planting schemes by carrying garden interest throughout the year. The evergreen plants shown here – climbing (or carpeting) *Hedera colchica* 'Sulphur Heart' *(left)* and glittering *Ilex × altaclarensis* 'Lawsoniana' *(right)* – both serve this purpose well.

***Hedera colchica* 'Sulphur Heart'** has large heart-shaped leaves splashed with golden yellow. It is a good evergreen climber to use in dark corners of the garden, where it will bring a warm glow all year round. Occasionally a whole leaf will be yellow and on older leaves the yellow may have a greenish tone. Any soil in sun or semi-shade will suffice.

Hedera helix is a species of small-leaved evergreen ivy with a long list of cultivars, many of them variegated white or yellow. Of the latter, 'Goldchild' is probably one of the best with its bright green leaves splashed with pale green in the centre surrounded by a golden yellow margin. Increase from layers or cuttings taken in late summer. It requires moisture-retentive soil in semi-shade.

***Ilex × altaclarensis* 'Lawsoniana'** A large shrub or medium-sized tree with brightly coloured large spineless leaves splashed with yellow in the centre. Alternatively, *I. × a.* 'Golden King' has broad green almost spineless leaves with a yellow margin and *I. × a.* 'Belgica Aurea' has flat deep green leaves with a creamy yellow margin. Any soil in sun.

***Rosmarinus officinalis* 'Aureus'** is the gilded rosemary treasured in the cottage and knot gardens and parterres of earlier centuries. Rosemary is generally a splendid evergreen shrub – there are prostrate forms, weeping forms and white- and pink-flowered cultivars, all smelling and tasting delicious – but the gold-splashed variegations of the gilded rosemary make it particularly special. It is not fully hardy, so give it a sheltered spot or else overwinter it under glass. Propagate from semi-ripe cuttings in summer. It requires a well-drained soil in sun.

WHITE-VARIEGATED

White variegation appears less showy than yellow; perhaps because it blends more easily with the soft pastel shades of spring and early summer. *Arum italicum* 'Marmoratum' appears as the first bulbs begin to push through.

Ornamental brassicas make a terrific annual display for the winter garden and the F1 hybrid mixes offered by seed merchants give you selections of ruff-leaved cabbages and spider-lace kale in shades of pink, carmine and, most spectacularly, white.

Annuals and perennials

Arum italicum **'Marmoratum'** (lords and ladies) When most other foliage plants are losing their glamour in autumn this herbaceous perennial begins to put on a show, sending up large, glossy, arrowhead-shaped leaves deeply veined in silvery white. Use with hellebores and other winter- and early spring-flowering plants. Propagate by division after the leaves have faded away or just as they begin to emerge. There will be plenty of self-sown seedlings as well to increase your stock.

Plant in moisture-retentive soil in sun or semi-shade.

Arundo donax **'Variegata'** (syn. *A. d.* var. *versicolor*) For a bold exclamation point this stately perennial grass can hardly be bettered. Erect stems well above the height of the average adult carry narrow strappy leaves variegated in bold white stripes. It is not hardy so must be overwintered under glass, but is well worth the effort. An essential ingredient of the tropical border. Site in moisture-retentive soil in sun and propagate by division in spring.

Brassica oleracea provides gardeners with ornamental cabbage and kale as well as nourishing 'greens'. Most seed catalogues now list these frilly fancies, with shades of creamy white, pink and mauve brightening the crunchy leaves. Grow as for winter cabbages, then plant out into the garden or, best of all, fill containers with bouquets of them. Sow the seed in early summer in a seedbed and then prick out into individual pots. Pot on as the plants develop and feed well to achieve really spectacular plants. They will thrive in any soil. Added lime benefits growth.

In some foliage plants, the variegation emphasizes the shape or structure of the leaves: the curves and undulations
of *Hosta undulata* var. *unirittata (above)* are enhanced by the bold splash of white variegation. just as the slender leaves
of *Miscanthus sinensis* 'Malepartus' *(opposite above)* look even skinnier because of the single white central stripe.
Some variegation. however. will simply frost each leaf with silver. as in the annual *Lunaria annua* 'Alba Variegata'
(opposite below).

Carex spp. *C. oshimensis* grows to about 30cm (12in) and has much broader leaves than other *Carex* species. It has an equally bright variegation with each leaf boldly edged in white: the form 'Evergold' is edged in clotted-cream yellow. When this perennial grass is planted in large groups the variegation creates a shimmering effect like light on the surface of the sea. *Carex siderosticha* 'Variegata' is a stunning specimen plant with broad white-variegated leaves: it makes a graceful mound composed of long ribbon-like leaves. each one clearly edged in white. It is a perennial plant which grows to about 45cm (18in). Propagate by division in the spring and plant in a moisture-retentive soil in sun or semi-shade.

Hosta undulata var. unirittata This is a hardy perennial with undulate leaves carrying a central white stripe of variegation. Over the years the plant becomes less variegated eventually reverting to green. Propagate by division. Plant in shade in a rich moisture-retentive soil.

Lunaria annua 'Alba Variegata' (honesty) A quick-growing biennial with variegated coarse-toothed. heart-shaped leaves. Propagate by seed. Plant in a well-drained soil in semi-shade.

Miscanthus sinensis I have picked this particular species of *Miscanthus* because it gives the most choice of garden varieties and is easy to grow. It also offers some good specimen plants for the border or garden when you need something other than a shrub and the flowers are quite showy for a grass. in some varieties appearing quite late in the autumn. The broad leaves of 'Malepartus' are enhanced by a thin white central stripe

Phalaris arundinacea 'Picta' *(left)*, better known as gardener's garters, is flashier than many white-variegated plants, but is incredibly invasive, especially in moisture-retentive soils; the sort known as 'Feesey's Form' is less troublesome and has even stronger, whiter markings.

while 'Silberfeder' (or 'Silverfeather') grows to at least 2.4m (8ft) when well suited and is topped with gloriously silky flowerheads that glisten in the breeze of a sunny autumn day. 'Variegatus' is widely available, with leaves having a broad white stripe variegation; 'Zebrinus' is cream variegated with horizontal stripes across the leaf blade rather than along it. 'Morning Light' has the silvery effect of 'Silberfeder' enhanced by a broad white stripe along the leaf margins. Propagate by division in spring. Give it moisture-retentive soil in sun or semi-shade.

***Persicaria virginiana* 'Painter's Palette'** *(syn. Tovara virginiana* 'Painter's Palette') is a low-growing hardy perennial forming loose mounds of oval mid-green foliage splashed with cream and marked with a garnet-red chevron across each leaf. This colour is echoed on the stems, giving the plant a rather reddish cast. Plant in moisture-retentive soil in sun and propagate by division.

***Phalaris arundinacea* 'Picta'** is a perennial grass with broad white-striped leaves which taper to a point. This plant

can be invasive. Propagate by division. Plant in any soil in the sun.

***Pulmonaria* spp. and cultivars** (lungwort) There are dozens of species and named cultivars of this familiar cottage garden herb bearing varying degrees of silvery markings on long, tapering leaves with a slightly rough texture. *P. rubra* 'David Ward' has soft grey-green colouring and bold creamy-white variegation; *P. longifolia* 'Bertram Anderson' has long narrow leaves and glittering spots of silver that are especially bright in autumn; and *P. saccharata*

The heavily variegated oval leaves of the lungwort *Pulmonaria saccharata* Argentea Group *(centre)* are at their best in spring. Splashed with varying degrees of silver, they are a perfect foil for spring flower colour among hellebores, narcissus and primroses. The white markings of the climber *Actinida kolomikta (right)* are tinged with sunburn pink; always buy a plant in leaf to be sure of having good variegation – some plants perform better than others.

Argentea Group has heavily silvered leaves mottled with dark grey-green. Pulmonarias are supremely collectible, and are good clump-formers to use as ground cover among spring-flowering plants, hellebores and heucheras. Propagate by division in autumn. They like moisture-retentive soil in semi-shade.

Shrubs and climbers

Actinidia kolomikta is a vigorous twining climber with broad, vaguely heart-shaped deciduous leaves that are splashed at the tips with white and pink:

sometimes the entire leaf will show little evidence of green. However, plants will not show variegation until mature. Small fragrant white flowers open in early summer. This climber can be propagated by layering or internodal cuttings and will grow in any soil in full sun.

Hedera colchica '**Dentata Variegata**' is an evergreen ivy with large heart-shaped leaves edged in creamy white. Use it to clothe fences and decorate walls or else as groundcover to create a bright carpet for spring bulbs to show through: it will grow in any soil in sun or semi-shade.

Trees

Cornus controversa '**Variegata**' It is worth spending a little extra to obtain the best specimen you can of this splendid tree and then give it the best treatment you can. The reward will be a stunning display of tiered branches covered in bright silvery variegation. Let it be one of the stars of the garden by giving it a place centre stage. In autumn the leaves often turn a rich purple-red. A medium-sized deciduous tree, it likes well-drained soil in sun or semi-shade.

AUTUMN COLOUR

The rusty leaves of the sedge *Carex comans* bronze are a curious mix of khaki-green and brick-red. As the seasons pass
the leaves fade from their tips to a warm biscuit brown in autumn and retain this soft colouring throughout winter.

Euphorbias provide gardeners with a huge range of colour, texture, form and habit from which to choose. There are tiny-leaved wine-red sorts and others with bright green needle-like leaves. Some have erect stems, while there are many lax, mound-forming varieties. They contribute to the scene all year round, but autumn particularly benefits, especially from *Euphorbia griffithii* 'Fireglow'.

Annuals and perennials

Carex **spp.** There are nearly 2000 species of this sedge and among them are some stunning perennial foliage plants providing shades of cinnamon brown, brassy green and bright yellow and white variegations. Although they retain their colour all year round it is of particular value in autumn when most perennials are past their best. *C. buchananii* is erect, growing to about 60cm (2ft), and has glossy copper foliage that can make sudden loose corkscrew curls at the tips; *C. comans*

bronze only grows to about 25cm (10in) and makes a soft spreading tuft of rather glossy leaves tinted pale cordovan brown – stunning planted in ribbons through a border. Propagate by division in spring and site in moisture-retentive soil in sun or semi-shade.

Euphorbia **spp. and cultivars** This genus of evergreen perennials provides some of the finest 'feature' plants in the garden – the sort of plant you place in eye-catching positions or else use as markers in the scheme of things. While they look good for most of the year. I

think they really come into their own in the autumn. They are available in a wide range of sizes, from the small ground-covering *E. cyparissias* with short, limp stems covered in pale green leaves resembling bottle brushes to the large and widely grown *E. characias* ssp. *wulfenii*, which has erect stems covered in glaucous blue-green narrow leaves topped by whorls of lime-green flower bracts. In between, *E. × martinii* has a similar habit of upright growth but red-tinged stems and leaves. Other red euphorbias are *E. griffithii* 'Dixter', which has a particularly dense colour.

An uncommon member of the ubiquitous cotoneaster clan is *Cotoneaster lancasterii (left)*, seen here at Saling Hall in Essex. The mix of fiery red, gold and silver-backed leaves makes this a splendid shrub for the autumn border. Plants of the Monticola Group of *Fothergilla major (centre)* have the characteristic white bottle-brush flowers on naked stems, but only after the shrub has shed its glorious fireflame autumn raiment.

E. g. 'Fireglow' and *E. dulcis* 'Chameleon', which is almost entirely dark burgundy red, with the hint of green about it equally murky. It makes a good clump of foliage among spring-flowering plants. *E. seguieriana* ssp. *niciciana* has arching stems of stubby blue-grey leaves. Propagate from cuttings in late summer or else by division (or self-sown seedlings in the case of *E. dulcis* 'Chameleon'). They require well-drained soil in sun or semi-shade.

***Geranium macrorrhizum* 'Album'** is the white-flowered cultivar of this hardy geranium which is best loved for the resin-scented foliage that takes on rust-red and purple tones during autumn. It is easily propagated by cuttings taken throughout summer or by division and will grow in any soil in sun.

Shrubs and climbers

Cotoneaster lancasterii Most members of this genus have something to offer but for bold autumn colour, this species is worth searching for. Propagate by semi-ripe cuttings. Plant in any soil in sun or part shade.

Fothergilla (witch alder) *F. gardenii* makes a rounded mound of soft blue-green foliage that turns fiery orange in autumn; in spring the naked branches bear dense clusters of scented white flowers. *F. g.* 'Blue Mist' is a widely available cultivar that colours well and *F. major* makes an upright shrub bearing fluffy white scented flowers on naked branches during mid- to late spring. The serrate oval leaves are a rather dull grey-green, turning to excellent shades of gold and scarlet in autumn. Propagate from semi-ripe cuttings in late summer. These

Parthenocissus tricuspidata (right), better known as Boston ivy, is the mournful cladding of many a late-nineteenth-century building, shrouding every architectural detail in a mantle of flat green. However, the autumn colour can be spectacular: 'Veitchii' becomes dark burgundy purple and 'Lowii' has deeply cut and frilled edges.

medium-sized deciduous shrubs do best on acid moisture-retentive soil in semi-shade.

Hamamelis mollis is the witch hazel, a deciduous large shrub or small tree which is beautiful all year round. In early spring the branches are alive with delicately perfumed flowers which are replaced by heavily textured, broad, rounded leaves that turn golden yellow in autumn. The habit is broad and spreading and the plant matures slowly. It prefers acid soil but will grow in any good well-drained soil in semi-shade.

Parthenocissus quinquefolia (Virginia creeper), although more widely grown, is less interesting than *P. henryana*, which has leaves comprising three to five leaflets with a soft matt surface veined in palest pink or white remaining prominent even when the foliage has taken on the rich ruby tints of autumn. *P. tricuspidata*, however, has a shorter moment of autumn glory when its broad-lobed leaves, with a glossy surface, colour a startling ruby-red; unfortunately during the rest of the year it can lack interest. Initially, all climb by tendrils, so walls should be fixed with

wires; they can also be used to clothe dull trees and brighten east- or north-facing aspects. Propagate from soft cuttings in summer. They like well-drained soil in full or semi-shade.

Viburnum spp. and cultivars provide the autumn and early spring garden with some good colour and textures; there are deciduous and evergreen sorts to choose from. *V. davidii* has dark green, slightly glossy, but heavily veined leaves, giving it a rough-looking texture; it makes a low, spreading evergreen shrub and there are male and female

Often mistaken for a maple because of its palmate leaves, *Liquidambar styraciflua (above)* also shares the brilliant autumn colouring – sometimes. Trees raised from cuttings of the clones 'Worplesdon' or 'Lane Roberts' are, however, sure-fire selections. The young growth of *Nyssa sinensis (below)* anticipates the bright red colouring of its autumn foliage.

of the pinnate foliage which makes the broad spreading tree look like a cloud of golden raindrops. It carries panicles of yellow flowers that turn to bladder-like fruit in late summer. A medium-sized deciduous tree, it will grow in any soil in sun. The cultivar 'Fastigiata' is a small tree with a tidy columnar habit.

Liquidambar styraciflua (sweet gum) This deciduous tree of medium size provides the most glorious autumn colours, from deep burgundy purple leaves on the lowest branches to sunburst yellow in the uppermost, or else

solidly wine red – it all depends on the tree and the soil, it seems. In my garden the young tree stayed a lacklustre browny green in its first few autumns, but now, eight years on, it gives me the most profound pleasure with lovely lingering ruby-red palmate leaves and an elegant conical habit. It requires moisture-retentive soils in sun or semi-shade and will not tolerate shallow chalk soils.

Nothofagus fusca (red beech) has glorious coppery tints in the autumn and on older trees the bark develops a flaking appearance. *N. solandri* (black

beech) is valued for the graceful way the tiny leaves gather in fan-like clusters on the wiry stems: *N. s.* var. *cliffortioides* is most easily available. Both of these small trees are New Zealand natives and are quite hardy, but appreciate shelter from strong winds. They require well-drained acid soil in sun or semi-shade.

***Nyssa* spp.** The glossy dark green foliage of *N. sylvatica,* the black gum or tupelo tree, gives spectacular blazing autumn colour. This medium-sized tree has a pleasing broad columnar habit, making it a good specimen tree for a

In early spring the young leaves of *Prunus sargentii* are a soft coppery red that offsets the pale pink flowers perfectly.
It makes a graceful tree with its broad spreading crown and, come early autumn, the foliage turns a deep crimson,
heralding the change of the season.

distant view. It is fairly slow-growing so takes a while to come into its own, and because it dislikes being transplanted it is best to buy a young tree. *N. sinensis* has narrowish leaves which change to a vibrant blend of vivid reds in autumn. Give them a moist soil in sun.

Parrotia persica (Persian ironwood) is a broadly spreading small deciduous tree with exceptionally hard wood. It is a relative of the witch hazel and shares that tree's graceful habit. In autumn, the long oval leaves colour golden yellow, touched with apple red at the tips. They

are quite slow-growing but a mature tree is a beautiful thing, especially when complemented by autumn-flowering *Cyclamen hederifolium*. It requires moisture-retentive soil in sun.

Populus tremuloides (quaking aspen) Like the bamboo *(see page 148)* this is a garden music-maker and the fluttering leaves create movement and sound in an open setting. The foliage colours a glorious golden yellow. This deciduous tree can grow to 30m (100ft), so it needs space and perspective to be appreciated. It prefers well-drained soil in sun.

Prunus sargentii (Sargent's cherry) has long, tapering oval leaves and a broad, upright, spreading crown. In spring there are pretty clusters of shell-pink flowers; during the summer the tree is simply green and leafy, but come autumn the foliage is among the first to turn gradually to shades of vermilion, ochre, chrome yellow and palest buttercup. This lasts for a few magnificent days, then the leaves drop all at once to the ground – still looking splendid. A small deciduous tree, it likes well-drained soil in sun and is good on chalk soils.

BARK, STEM & BERRY

Chusquea culeou is one of the most stately bamboos, referred to by one specialist grower as 'the cream of bamboos'.
The beautifully banded canes alone make it worth growing, with the arching sprays of fine foliage providing a perfect
counterpoint to its demanding visual presence.

Eryngium bourgatii 'Oxford Blue' is spectacular for its icy stem colouring that creeps into the bracts and seedheads. The old Edwardian favourite *E. × zabelii* is a hybrid of lavishly ruffed *E. alpinum* and *E. bourgatii*, so it has the lacy bracts of the first and the rich colouring of the latter.

Annuals and perennials

Briza maxima is commonly known as quaking grass because the delightful pendent spikelets dip and bob in the breeze; the inflorescence appears throughout summer followed by seedheads which turn a soft buff straw colour as they dry. An annual, it self-seeds freely. Divide in spring to increase stocks. *Briza* will grow in any soil in sun or semi-shade.

Chasmanthium latifolium has the most graceful inflorescence of any grass,

bearing panicles of thumbnail-sized flowers that look like flattened outsize oats dangling from the finest of stems. It is erect-growing to about 90cm (3ft), with drooping leaves widely spaced along the length of each stem. Site it where the movement of the panicles, which fade from pale green to biscuit brown, can be easily observed. Propagate by division in the spring. It requires well-drained soil in semi-shade.

Chusquea culeou (Chilean bamboo) is one of the best bamboos; it is very hardy, very large with canes up to 5m

(15ft) tall and forms dense clumps up to 3m (10ft) across.

Eryngium bourgatii '**Oxford Blue**' Tall multi-headed stems rise from a ground-hugging rosette of deeply cut and veined leaves. A metallic silver-blue sheen dominates the leaves, stem and teasel-like flowerheads. Propagate this perennial by division in the spring. Plant in a well-drained soil in a sunny position.

Eupatorium purpureum (Joe Pye weed) is a stately perennial with rather uninteresting whorls of foliage wrapped

The silvered canes of *Rubus cockburnianus (left)* make a bold statement in the winter garden when contrasted against
dark evergreens or among spring-flowering hellebores. The crimson bark of *Cornus alba* 'Sibirica' *(centre)* has a similarly
startling effect, so the winter garden need not lack colour interest.

around exceedingly tall erect red stems
that are topped by umbels of rosy-red
tubular flowers in late summer and early
autumn. It grows to 2m (6½ft) or more.
Propagate by division in autumn or
early spring and plant in well-drained
soil in semi-shade.

Hordeum jubatum Squirrel or fox-tail
barley is an annual or short-lived
perennial grass often seen growing wild in
roadside verges or in field margins,
singled out from the crowd by the
gracefully arching stems carrying long
feathery flower spikes that fade to

attractive seedheads. It will grow in any
well-drained soil in sun.

Pennisetum **spp. and cultivars** This
grass is valuable for the wonderful
fluffy seedheads rather than for the
loose tufts of limp foliage it produces.
P. alopecuroides sends up arching flower
stems in late summer that gradually
transform into long panicles of seeds,
each one tufted with long hairs, so that
the plant looks as if it is covered in
fuzzy caterpillars. *P. orientale* is much
more glamorous, with a longer panicle
and softer, silkier, pink-tinged hairs on

the seeds. *P. setaceum* is worth seeking
out for the red-tinged colour of the
entire plant. Propagate from seed or by
division in spring. Pennisetums prefer
light, warm soils in sun.

Phyllostachys **spp. and cultivars**
(bamboo) If, like me, you have no easy
source of water, I advise a stand of
bamboo sited where the breeze will stir
its leaves; the soft rustle is as pleasing as
that of any water feature. There are
quite a number of *Phyllostachys* species,
some of which have distinctly colourful
and curiously shaped stems that can add

Cornus stolonifera 'Flaviramea' *(right)* joins the other dogwoods in providing a vivacious colour during the dull winter months. The finest hue on all such shrubs appears on new wood, so it is important to cut out old growth each spring to encourage new shoots for winter interest.

verticality to a planting scheme. *P. aurea* 'Flavescens Inversa' carries a yellow groove along the internodal segments of the sturdy green stems, or culms, while *P. bambusoides* 'Castilloni' has green grooves on straw-yellow culms; *P. nigra* has brownish-black culms, and *P. n.* 'Boryana' displays splashes of inky brown along them. *P. violascens* acquires purplish-green markings as it ages. Apply a mulch of well-rotted compost annually to help conserve moisture and occasionally thin out old stems to allow warm summer sun to penetrate to their hearts.

Propagate by division of the clumps. These evergreen perennials like moisture-retentive soil in sun or semi-shade.

Rubus spp. Recommended are *R. cock-burnianus* with blue-white stems in winter, *R. phoenicolasius* (Japanese wineberry), with ruby-red heavily prickled stems and bright green leaves with silvered under-sides, and *R. thibetanus*, much the most refined member of the family, with silvery feathery foliage and long, arching, waxy-white stems. Like all brambles they do run about, but are easily controlled by chopping out chunks.

They are hardy perennials that will thrive in any soil in sun.

Shrubs and climbers

Cornus spp. *C. alba* (red-stem dogwood) is a vigorous medium-sized deciduous shrub with an upright habit, spreading into a rounded shape with age. The simple oval-shaped foliage colours well and brightly coloured bark enhances young stems during winter. Shrubs grown for this effect should be positioned in full sun and cut back hard in spring. 'Aurea' has soft yellow foliage;

The tidy linear structure of *Cotoneaster horizontalis (above)* is emphasized by the tiny crimson berries snug amid diminutive leaves; this plant makes excellent wall cover or groundcover beneath shrubs and hedges. *Pyracantha* 'Orange Glow' *(below left)* is widely grown as a wall-trained shrub, covered in spring with clusters of white flowers, replaced by orange berries in autumn. *Rosa rugosa* 'Scabrosa' *(below right)* is another suckering shrub with bright fruit and also autumn colouring: it provides good hedging in difficult conditions, like seaside gardens and dry shade.

in 'Elegantissima' the soft green leaves are mottled and edged with white: 'Kesselringii' has dark green leaves deepening to claret red in autumn on dark purple stems: 'Sibirica' has fiery crimson stems in winter: and 'Spaethii' has leaves variegated yellow. *Cornus stolonifera* 'Flaviramea' has bright green-yellow bark in winter. Propagate from semi-ripe cuttings in late summer and plant in moisture-retentive to moist soil in sun or semi-shade.

Corylus avellana 'Contorta' This medium-sized deciduous shrub really

only comes into its own in late maturity when it has the substance and height to carry off the oddly twisted branches and stems. The leaves carry the same distortion. so it looks rather a mess until leaf-drop. but bare stems and catkins together make a remarkable show. Propagate from semi-ripe cuttings taken in late summer. It will grow in any soil in sun or semi-shade.

Cotoneaster spp. There are dozens of cotoneasters and most are valued for their colourful berries in shades of red. orange and yellow. Some species

(*C. horizontalis* in particular) will self-sow. Ranked according to leaf size, large to small. species and forms worth looking out for are: *C. bullatus. C. frigidus* 'Cornubia'. *C. dammeri. C. frigidus. C. salicifolius* 'Rothschildianus'. *C. × watereri* 'John Waterer'. *C. conspicuus* 'Decorus'. *C. horizontalis. C. microphyllus* and *C. nitidus*. Propagate from semi-ripe cuttings in late summer. These medium to groundcovering shrubs will grow in any soil in sun or semi-shade.

Pyracantha spp. and cultivars (firethorn) These evergreen shrubs are

Symphoricarpos albus is aptly known as the snowberry: it is a common shrub that can make a suckering thicket so is often used as boundary hedge in its native North America.

most often grown as wall-trained specimens. Despite their pleasing tiny glossy leaves it is their berries which make them noteworthy, coming in shades of red, orange and yellow. *P.* 'Orange Glow' and *P.* 'Golden Charmer' describe themselves: *P.* 'Watereri' has a compact habit and bright red fruit; *P. rogersiana* 'Flava' has narrow dull green leaves but vibrant yellow berries; *P. atalantioides* has large glossy leaves and long-lasting clusters of bright red berries. Increase from cuttings taken in late summer and plant in well-drained soil in sun or semi-shade.

***Rosa* spp. and cultivars** A good many roses provide interesting stems and/or good autumn colour from leaves and hips. The latter can be as round as golf balls or long and tapering like little bottles. *R. rugosa* 'Scabrosa' comes to mind for its exceptional large, glowing red globes of seed-filled hips. In early autumn this is a marvellous spectacle with golden leaves, red hips and spicily perfumed bright pink flowers appearing all at once. *R.* 'Blanche Double de Coubert' makes a tall leggy shrub if left to itself, and in autumn the branches are covered in butter-yellow leaves that last

well into early winter. *R. foliolosa* makes a lax shrub with red-tinged stems and a dressing of pinnate leaves. It also has clusters of rusty-red hips. *R. californica* 'Plena' makes an upright spreading shrub covered in clusters of starry flowers followed by masses of crimson hips amid the yellowing leaves. Provide with a well-drained soil and a sunny position.

Symphoricarpos albus A deciduous shrub bearing white to pink berries in autumn and winter. Plant in any well-drained soil in sun or shade. Propagate by division of suckers.

Specimen trees can be chosen for many reasons, and bark quality and character are high on the list. Many maples have good texture and colour, like *Acer forestii* 'Alice' *(left)* with its corrugated cordovan-coloured bark. Birch, too, is well-loved as a feature tree, and *Betula ermanii (right)* displays the blotched whiteness characteristic of these trees.

Trees

Acer **spp.** *A. forestii* 'Alice' is a small deciduous tree with striated bark which when young is a pretty coral-red. *A. griseum* is the paperbark maple, so called for its ginger-red peeling bark; plant it where the light will shine through the papery film. *A. capillipes* (snakebark maple) has a trunk marked with silvery-green striations. These deciduous trees thrive in any soil in sun or semi-shade.

Arbutus unedo This is known commonly as the strawberry tree on account of the bright red glossy fruit which, sadly, has no taste. Mature trees have superb Titian-red bark, smooth and pleasingly tactile, and glossy green foliage, making this a perfect medium-sized evergreen specimen tree. Give it shelter in cold gardens or raise it in a large tub. It requires well-drained soil in sun.

Betula pendula 'Youngii', *B. jacque-montii* and *B. ermanii* 'Grayswood Hill' are best for ghostly white bark effects. These are medium-sized deciduous trees and a stand of them artfully placed to catch the setting sun is one of the great visual pleasures. Often the foliage will turn a pleasing buttery yellow in autumn. Site them in any soil in sun.

Calocedrus decurrens The incense cedar is one of the best trees for providing a vertical accent; the fan-shaped fronds fold themselves around the trunk, which is sheathed in pleasing scented red-tinged bark. It makes a large evergreen tree and will grow in any soil in sun.

Eucalyptus **spp.** These are fast-growing evergreen trees with lush foliage and attractive stems and trunks *(see page*

The bark of the snow gum, *Eucalyptus pauciflora (left)*, is typical of the elegant colours and textures these antipodean natives share; combined with the grey-green foliage they have a pale spectral presence in the garden unlike the rugged stone pine, *Pinus pinea (right)*, with its bold outline and heavily modelled bark textures.

127). *E. pauciflora* (snow gum) has a lovely snakeskin bark of green, grey and cream. *E. johnstonii* (yellow gum) is a large tree with reddish bark. Avoid shallow soil over chalk and plant in a sheltered position in sun or semi-shade.

***Pinus* spp.** *P. pinea* (stone pine or umbrella pine) is a distinct medium-sized tree with a flat-topped head and reddish bark. *P. densiflora* 'Umbraculifera' is the most interesting cultivar of the Japanese red pine. It grows only to about 3m (10ft) but will eventually make a gracefully shaped

dome spreading to twice that size. The branches are dark and sinuous, giving the tree a distinctive shape rather like that seen on blue willow pattern china. *P. bungeana* (lacebark pine) is a large shrub or small tree which has a pale grey-green bark that flakes to create a camouflage effect. These evergreens will grow in any soil in sun or semi-shade.

***Prunus* spp.** *P. serrula* is noted for its shiny peeling oxblood-red bark. In my garden I encourage visitors to strip off the bark to reveal the glossy new layers underneath. It will grow in any soil in

sun and is good on chalk soils. *Prunus* 'Taihaku' is also known as the great white cherry, much loved by Vita Sackville-West. There are few cherries which give a more breathtaking show: in early spring the foliage begins to appear as little bright green wings tinged with cherry red, followed by pendent clusters of pure white flowers. It makes a broad, upright spreading crown in maturity, but even the young trees have a pleasing outline. In autumn the foliage colours a lingering rust-red and gold. A medium-sized deciduous tree, it will grow in any soil in sun and is good on chalk soils.

Plant site list

A guide to the siting of Plant Directory plants. Some entries may appear in more than one category.

Moisture-retentive soil in sun

Abies spp.

Acer palmatum and vars.

Arundo donax 'Variegata'

Carex spp.

Cercis canadensis

Cornus spp.

Cotinus spp.

Gunnera manicata

Houttuynia cordata 'Chameleon'

Liquidambar styraciflua

Lysichiton camtschatcensis

Miscanthus sinensis

Molina caerula ssp. *caerula* 'Variegata'

Musa basjoo and *M. acuminata*

Nyssa sylvatica

Parrotia persica

Persicaria virginiana 'Painter's Palette'

Phyllostachys spp. and cultivars

Ricinus communis

Rodgersia podophylla

Salix lanata

Zantedeschia aethiopica 'Crowborough'

Moisture-retentive soil in shade or semi-shade

Adiantum venustum

Ajuga reptans

Arum italicum 'Marmoratum'

Astilboides tabularis

Asplenium scolopendrium

Athyrium niponicum var. *pictum*

Carex spp.

Cornus spp.

Dicksonia antarctica

Filipendula ulmaria 'Aurea'

Fothergilla spp.

Gunnera manicata

Hakonechloa macra

Hedera helix vars.

Hosta spp. and cultivars

Houttuynia cordata 'Chameleon'

Hydrangea sargentiana

Liquidambar styraciflua

Lysichiton camtschatcensis and *L. americanus*

Lysimachia nummularia 'Aurea'

Matteuccia struthiopteris

Milium effusum 'Aureum'

Miscanthus sinensis

Phyllostachys spp. and cultivars

Polystichum setiferum

Pulmonaria spp. and cultivars

Veratrum nigrum

Viburnum spp. and cultivars

Zantedeschia aethiopica 'Crowborough'

Well-drained soil in sun

Acanthus spp.

Agave spp.

Arbutus unedo

Artemisia ludoviciana 'Silver Queen'

Aruncus dioicus 'Kneiffii'

Berberis thunbergii 'Red Pillar'

Canna musifolia 'Striata'

Cordyline australis

Cornus controversa 'Variegata'

Cryptomeria japonica 'Globosa Nana'

Cupressus sempervirens

Cynara cardunculus

Dudleya brittonii

Echeveria lindsayana

Elaeagnus angustifolia and *E.* x *ebbengei* 'Limelight'

Eryngium bourgatii 'Oxford Blue'

Eucalyptus spp.

Euphorbia spp. and cultivars

Festuca glauca

Ficus carica

Geranium sessiliflorum 'Nigricans'

Gleditsia triacanthos

Helictotrichon sempervirens

Helleborus x *sternii*

Hordeum jubatum

Juniperus spp.

Magnolia grandiflora

Melianthus major

Nandina domestica vars.

Nothofagus fusca

Ophiopogon planiscapus 'Nigrescens'

Origanum vulgare 'Aureum'

Pennisetum spp. and cultivars

Perilla frutescens

Perovskia atriplicifolia

Phormium tenax Purpureum Group

Acer palmatum 'Dissectum Atropurpureum'

Dicksonia antarctica

Stachys byzantina

Picea pungens glauca
Pinus wallichiana
Populus tremuloides
Prunus cerasifera 'Pissardii'
Prunus lusitanica
Prunus sargentii
Pyracantha spp. and cultivars
Pyrus salicifolia 'Pendula'
Quercus spp. and cultivars
Rosa spp. and cultivars
Rosmarinus officinalis 'Aureus'
Ruta graveolens
Salvia officinalis and cultivars
Sedum spp.
Stachys byzantina
Stipa spp.
Symphoricarpos albus
Thymus spp. and cultivars
Trachycarpus fortunei
Verbascum olympicum
Vitis spp. and cultivars

Well-drained soil in shade or semi-shade

Acanthus spp.
Aruncus dioicus 'Kneiffii'
Berberis thunbergii 'Red Pillar'
Chasmanthium latifolium
Cornus controversa 'Variegata'
Cryptomeria japonica 'Globosa Nana'
Elaeagnus angustifolia
Eupatorium purpureum
Euphorbia spp. and cultivars
Hamamelis mollis

Humulus lupulus 'Aureus'
Juniperus spp.
Lunaria annua 'Alba Variegata'
Nothofagus fusca
Ophiopogon planiscapus 'Nigrescens'
Parthenocissus quinquefolia
Phormium tenax 'Purpureum Group'
Picea pungens glauca
Prunus lusitanica
Pyracantha spp. and cultivars
Stachys byzantina
Symphoricarpos albus
Vitis spp. and cultivars

Any soil in shade or semi-shade

Acer spp
Alchemilla mollis
Alnus glutinosa 'Imperialis'
Astrantia major 'Sunningdale Variegated'
Azara microphylla
Brassica oleracea
Briza maxima
Corylus avellana 'Contorta'
Cotoneaster spp.
Hedera colchica 'Dentata Variegata'
Hedera colchica 'Sulphur Heart'
Ilex spp.
Pinus spp.
Taxus spp.
Vinca major 'Variegata'

Any soil in sun

Acer spp.

Actinidia kolomikta
Alchemilla mollis
Alnus glutinosa 'Imperialis'
Astrantia major 'Sunningdale Variegated'
Azara microphylla
Betula spp.
Brassica oleracea
Briza maxima
Calocedrus decurrens
Catalpa bignonioides 'Aurea'
Corylus avellana 'Contorta'
Cotoneaster spp.
Elymus magellanicus
Eriobotrya japonica
Fagus sylvatica 'Aspleniifolia' and 'Rohanii'
Geranium macrorrhizum 'Album'
Hedera colchica 'Dentata Variegata'
Hedera colchica 'Sulphur Heart'
Ilex spp.
Koeleria vallesiana
Koelreuteria paniculata
Lychnis coronaria
Phalaris arundinacea 'Picta'
Pinus spp
Prunus spp.
Rheum palmatum 'Atrosanguineum'
Robinia pseudoacacia 'Frisia'
Rosa rubrifolia
Rubus spp.
Taxus spp.
Vinca major 'Variegata'

Berberis thunbergii 'Red Pillar'

Alchemilla mollis

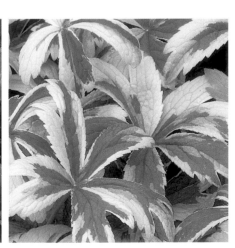

Astrantia major 'Sunningdale Variegated'

Where to see and buy foliage plants

UNITED KINGDOM

Abbotsbury Sub-Tropical Gardens, Abbotsbury, Nr Weymouth, Dorset DT3 4LA.
Less common and tender shrubs. Display gardens.

Altoona Nurseries, The Windmill, Tigley, Dartington, Totnes, Devon TQ9 6JT.
Japanese maples.

Apple Court, Hordle Lane, Hordle, Lymington, Hants, SO41 0HU.
Fine collection of ferns, grasses and hostas (holders of National Collection of hostas).

Architectural Plants, Cooks Farm, Nuthurst, Horsham, West Sussex, RH13 6LH.
Plants with particularly fine, structural foliage; hardy exotics.

The Beth Chatto Gardens Ltd, Elmstead Market, Colchester, Essex CO7 7DB.
Choice and unusual perennials for every situation. Display gardens.

Bosvigo Plants, Bosvigo House, Bosvigo Lane, Truro, Cornwall TR1 3NH.
Unusual and choice herbaceous plants. Display gardens.

Burncoose & Southdown Nurseries, Gwennap, Redruth, Cornwall TR16 6BJ.
Huge range of ornamental trees and shrubs. Display gardens.

Cally Gardens, Gatehouse of Fleet, Castle Douglas, Scotland, DG7 2DJ.
An unusual collection of perennials, euphorbias, hardy geraniums and grasses; rare shrubs, climbers, and conservatory plants.

Daleside Nurseries, Ripon Rd, Killinghall, Harrogate, North Yorks HG3 2AY.
Selection of unusual trees and shrubs.

Denmans Garden (John Brookes Ltd), Clock House, Denmans, Fontwell, Nr Arundel, West Sussex, BN18 0SU.
Rare and unusual plants, many for fine foliage. Display gardens.

Drysdale Garden Exotics, Bowerwood Road, Fordingbridge, Hants SP6 1BN.
Foliage and exotic plants; plants for Mediterranean-style gardens.

Sedum spectabile 'Autumn Joy'

Foliage and Unusual Plants, Dingle Plants and Gardens, Stamford Road, Pilsgate, Stamford, Lincs PE9 3HW.
Plants selected especially for their foliage.

Glebe Cottage Plants, Pixie Lane, Warkleigh, Umberleigh, North Devon, EX37 9DH.
Rare and unusual herbaceous perennials.

Goldbrook Plants, Hoxne, Eye, Suffolk, IP21 5AN.
Perennials, grasses and extensive range of hostas.

Green Farm Plants, Bury Court, Bentley, Farnham, Surrey, GU10 5JX.
Specialists in a wide range of hardy border plants, many uncommon. Display garden designed by leading European plantsman, Piet Oudolf.

Hadspen Garden and Nursery, Hadspen House, Castle Cary, Somerset BA7 7NG.
Wide selection of good foliage perennials. Display gardens.

Harlow Carr Gardens, Harrogate, North Yorks.
Display gardens of the Northern Horticultural Society. Plants for sale.

Heldon Nurseries, Ashbourne Road, Spath, Uttoxeter, Staffs ST14 5AD.
Cacti and succulents.

Hergest Croft Gardens, Kington, Herefordshire HR5 3EG.
Unusual woody plants; Acer and Betula a speciality.

Herterton House Garden Nursery, Hartington, Cambo, Morpeth, Northumberland, NE61 4BN.
Wide range of unusual herbaceous plants grown in open ground, many collected by owners, Frank and Marjorie Lawley. Breath-taking display gardens.

Brian Hiley, 25 Little Woodcote Estate, Wallington, Surrey, SM5 4AU.
Half-hardy and tender exotics; herbaceous plants.

Hoecroft Plants, Severals Grange, Holt Road, Wood Norton, Dereham, Norfolk, NR20 5BL.
Specialists in grasses and plants with good foliage.

Hopleys Plants Ltd, High Street, Much Hadham, Herts SG10 6BU.
Good range of shrubs and herbaceous foliage plants. Display gardens.

Madrona Nursery, Pluckley Road, Bethersden, Kent TN26 3DD.
Unusual perennials, shrubs and conifers.

Mallet Court Nursery, Curry Mallet, Taunton, Somerset, TA3 6SY.
Hollies, maples, oaks and many rare and unusual trees and shrubs.

Monksilver Nursery, Oakington Road, Cottenham, Cambridgeshire, CB4 4TW.
Grasses, sedges, variegated and unusual plants.

Northumbria Nurseries, Castle Gardens, Ford, Berwick-upon-Tweed, Northumberland, TD15 2PZ.
Extensive selection of container-grown ornamental trees, shrubs and perennials

PW Plants, Sunnyside, Heath Road, Kenninghall, Norfolk, NR16 2DS.
Grasses, bamboos (a speciality) and an extensive range of good foliage plants.

The Palm Centre, 563 Upper Richmond Road West, London SW14 7ED.
Exotic and tropical, hardy and half-hardy plants; palms and cycads.

Pantiles Nurseries Ltd, Almners Road, Chertsey, Surrey, KT16 0BJ.
Australasian and other unusual plants; many trees, shrubs and climbers, container grown.

Rainbow's End Nursery, 37 Melbourn Road, Crookes, Sheffield, S10 1NR.
Black & white forms of herbaceous plants.

Reads Nursery, Hales Hall, Loddon, Norfolk, NR14 6QW.
Specialize in conservatory plants, wall shrubs and climbers, scented and aromatic hardy plants.

The Romantic Garden, Swannington, Norwich, Norfolk, NR9 5NW.
Topiary specialists and wide range of conservatory plants.

Trevor Scott, Thorpe Park Cottage, Thorpe-le-Soken, Essex, CO16 0HN.
Extensive range of ornamental grasses.

Seaforde Gardens, Seaforde, Co., Down, N. Ireland, BT30 8PG.
Wide range of nursery-propagated trees and shrubs.

Rosa rugosa 'Scabrosa'

Stapeley Water Gardens Ltd, London Road, Stapeley, Nantwich, Cheshire, CW5 7LH.
Water and bog plants.

Stydd Nursery, Stoneygate Lane, Ribchester, Nr Preston, Lancs, PR3 3YN.
Ornamental foliage plants; hardy and half-hardy perennials.

Washfield Nursery, Hawkhurst, Kent, TN18 4QU.
Choice and unusual alpine, perennial and woodland plants.

FRANCE

Etablissements Lepage, La Fontaine, Chemin des Perrins, 49130 Les-Ponts-de-Ce.

La Ferme Fleurie, 62270 Boubiers-sur-Canche.

Les Jardins d'en Face, La Ville du Monnier, 36730 Pleurtuit.

ITALY

Venzano, Loc. Venzano, Mazzola, 56048 Volterra (PI).
Specializes in aromatic and perfumed plants.

NETHERLANDS

Bulkyard Plants, Postbus 56, 2770 AB Boskoop.
A wide selection of shrubs.

Firma C. Esveld, Rijneveld 72, 2771 XS Boskoop.
An extensive list of trees and shrubs.

Kwekerij 'De Hessenhof', Hessenweg 41, 6718 TC Ede.
Specialize in ferns and woodland plants.

Kwekerij Oudolf, Broekstraat 17, 6999 de Hummelo.
Piet Oudolf's nursery and display garden. One of Europe's leading plantsmen, he has introduced a number of excellent perennials and grasses.

Jos van der Palen, Sandbergstraat 14, 5555 LB Valjkenswaard.
Bamboo and grass specialist nursery.

Pieter Zwijnenburg Jr., Halve Raak 18, 2771 AD Boskoop.
Shrubs specialist; also bamboos and a wide range of perennials.

Index

Bibliography

Aden, Paul ed. *The Hosta Book*, Timber Press 1995 (p/b 2nd ed)

Chatto, Beth, *The Green Tapestry*, Harper Collins 1989; *The Dry Garden*, Dent 1988 (p/b ed)

Druse, Ken *The Natural Habitat Garden*, Clarkson Potter 1994

Grenfell, Diana *The Gardener's Guide to Growing Hostas*, David & Charles 1996

Grounds, Roger, *Ornamental Grasses*, Christopher Helm 1989; *Ferns*, Pelham Books 1974

Hansen, Richard & Friedrich Stahl, *Perennials and Their Garden Habitats*, Cambridge Univ. Press 1993 (4th ed) trans.Richard Ward

Kelly, John ed. *The Hillier Gardener's Guide to Trees and Shrubs*, David & Charles 1995

Lloyd, Christopher, *Foliage Plants*, Penguin 1987 (revised p/b ed)

Rakusen, Pippa, *Foliage and Form Throughout the Year*, available only from Harlow Carr Botanical Gardens, Crag Lane, Harrogate, N. Yorks HG3 1QB.

Rix, Martyn & Roger Phillips, *Shrubs*, Macmillan 1989

Rose, Peter Q. *The Gardener's Guide to Growing Ivies*, David & Charles 1996

Thorpe, Patricia, *Growing Pains*, Harcourt Brace 1994

Underwood, Mrs Desmond, *Grey and Silver Plants*, Collins 1971

Verey, Rosemary, *The Garden in Winter*, Frances Lincoln 1988

Vertrees, J.D., *Japanese Maples*, Timber Press 1987 (2nd ed)

Yang, Linda *The City and Town Gardener*, Random House 1990

Picture Acknowledgements

Brian Carter/Garden Picture Library 114 (right); David England/Garden Picture Library 115 (right); John Glover/Garden Picture Library 115 (left), 112

Clive Nichols would like to acknowledge the kind cooperation of the designers, organizations and owners who gave permission to photograph the pictures on the following pages: 7 Preen Manor, Shropshire; 11 Herterton House, Northumberland; 12 High Beeches Garden, West Sussex; 13 The Sir Harold Hillier Gardens and Arboretum, Hampshire; 15 Bourton House, Gloucestershire; 16 Designer Olivia Clark; 17 Designer Jill Billington; 18 Hatfield House, Hertfordshire; 19 Wollerton Old Hall, Shropshire; 20 Designer Olivia Clark; 21 (left) La Casella, France (right) The Huntington Botanical Gardens; 23 Harcourt Arboretum, Oxfordshire; 26 City of Bath Botanical Gardens; 27 Ling Beeches, Yorkshire; 28 (left) Designer Sheila Jackson, London (right) Designer Sharon Osmond, San Francisco, California; 29 Herterton House, Cambo, Northumberland; 32 Winkworth Arboretum, Surrey; 34 (below left) Ling Beeches, Yorkshire; 35 (below left) Ling Beeches, Yorkshire (right) Spinners, Hampshire; 36 The Royal Horticultural Society's Garden, Wisley, Surrey; 37 The Manor House, Walton-in-Gordano, Bristol; 38 (left) Chenies Manor House, Buckinghamshire (right) Designer Olivia Clark; 40 (left) Longacre, Kent; 41 Designer Rupert Golby; 42 The Herb Farm, Sonning, Berkshire; 44 Ling Beeches, Yorkshire; 49 The Dingle, Welshpool, Powys; 51 The Valley Gardens, Surrey; 52-55 Wollerton Old Hall, Shropshire; 61 The Old Rectory, Sudborough Northamptonshire; 66-69 Hadspen House Garden and Nursery, Designers Sandra and Nori Pope; 77 Lower House Farm, Gwent; 79 The Dingle, Welshpool, Powys.